DOVER·THRIFT·EDITIONS

Metaphysical Poetry
An Anthology

EDITED BY
PAUL NEGRI

DOVER PUBLICATIONS, INC.
Mineola, New York

DOVER THRIFT EDITIONS

GENERAL EDITOR: PAUL NEGRI

EDITOR OF THIS VOLUME: THOMAS CRAWFORD

Bibliographical Note

Metaphysical Poetry: An Anthology is a new work, first published by Dover Publications, Inc., in 2002.

Library of Congress Cataloging-in-Publication Data

Metaphysical poetry : an anthology / edited by Paul Negri.
   p. cm.
   Contents: John Donne, 1572–1631 — Andrew Marvell, 1621–1678 — George Herbert, 1593–1633 — Richard Crashaw, 1613–1649 — Henry Vaughan, 1621–1695 — Thomas Traherne, 1637–1673
   ISBN 0-486-41916-9 (pbk.)
   1. English poetry—Early modern, 1500–1700. 2. Metaphysics—Poetry. I. Negri, Paul.

PR1209 .M49 2002
821'.309—dc21   2002073334

Manufactured in the United States of America
Dover Publications, Inc., 31 East 2nd Street, Mineola, N.Y. 11501

Dedicated to the memory of
Henry Searle

ঽ

And soonest our best men with thee do go,
Rest of their bones, and soul's delivery.

John Donne, *Death Be Not Proud*

Note

"About the beginning of the seventeenth century appeared a race of writers that may be termed metaphysical poets." —Dr. Samuel Johnson

Although Dr. Johnson used the term "metaphysical poet" in a disparaging sense, complaining that such poets as John Donne threw away their wit upon false conceits, i.e. yoking together dissimilar ideas in a violent fashion (*discordia concors*), he nevertheless acknowledged that the poets loosely grouped under the rubric "metaphysical" occasionally hit on unexpected truths. And if their conceits were far-fetched, they were sometimes worth the trouble. At the very least, their poetry required close reading and thinking.

By the end of the seventeenth century, however, the "metaphysical" poetry of Donne, George Herbert, Andrew Marvell and others had fallen out of favor and remained in obscurity for over two hundred years. It was not until modern times that metaphysical poetry was recognized for its true genius, in large part due to T. S. Eliot's famous and influential essay "The Metaphysical Poets" (1921). Eliot argued that metaphysical poetry fuses reason with passion, achieving a singular unification of thought and feeling which was lost in later verse, a negative development he termed a "dissociation of sensibility." As the noted critic and scholar H. J. C. Grierson points out (*Metaphysical Lyrics and Poems of the Seventeenth Century*, Oxford University Press, 1995), it is precisely their peculiar blend of passion and thought, feeling and ratiocination that is the greatest achievement of the metaphysical poets.

Encompassing a broad range of subjects, both sacred and secular, metaphysical poetry is characterized by wit (not humor as we think of it, but a nimbleness of thought and originality in figures of speech), its use of conceits–paradoxical metaphors which find likenesses in unlike things–irony, puns, and other word play. Often, metaphysical poems open with a dramatic, conversational ploy as in Herbert's "The Collar": "I struck the board and cry'd, No more," or Donne's "For God's sake hold your tongue, and let me love." These elements of ordinary speech are frequently mixed with learned terminology drawn from science or law, as well as neo-Platonic ideas about the relationship of the soul and the body, and human love in relation to the divine.

In general, metaphysical poetry offers a thought-provoking blend of the colloquial and the bizarre, full of vivid turns of phrase, abrupt rhythms and syntax, ingenious metaphors, and a pungent concentration of thought and sinewy strength of style. It is a poetry that invites the reader to join the poet in an intellectual and emotional adventure aimed at exploring the nature and felicities of love, both human and divine, the relationship of man to God, and the place and role of man in the universe.

Contents

Thomas Traherne (1637–1674)

JOHN DONNE (1572–1631)

Considered the greatest of the metaphysical poets, John Donne wrote both sacred and secular verse with equal facility. His secular poems — collected as *Songs and Sonnets* — explore the sensual and psychological elements of human love with wit, sophistication, intelligence, and immense poetic skill. Nevertheless, Dryden complained that Donne ". . . affects the metaphysics, not only in his satires, but in his amorous verses, where nature only should reign; and perplexes the minds of the fair sex with nice speculations of philosophy, when he should engage their hearts, and entertain them with the softnesses of love." Donne was far too much of a thinker to be content with appealing simply to the hearts of his readers; his poems engage the mind as well. Born a Roman Catholic, he attended both Oxford and Cambridge, but took no degrees, perhaps because of the oath of allegiance to the king required at graduation. In the 1590s Donne converted to Anglicanism, eventually becoming dean of St. Paul's Cathedral in 1621. His sermons, powerful and deeply moving, are considered among the most brilliant and eloquent of the age. In later years Donne turned this poetic genius to sacred verse, writing eloquent hymns and holy sonnets that conveyed the torment and hard-won grace of his spiritual struggles.

The Good Morrow

> I wonder by my troth, what thou, and I
> Did, till we loved? were we not weaned till then?
> But sucked on country pleasures, childishly?
> Or snorted we in the seven sleepers' den?
> 'Twas so; but this, all pleasures fancies be.
> If ever any beauty I did see,
> Which I desired, and got, 'twas but a dream of thee.

And now good morrow to our waking souls,
Which watch not one another out of fear;
For love, all love of other sights controls,
And makes one little room, an everywhere.
Let sea-discoverers to new worlds have gone,
Let maps to other, worlds on worlds have shown,
Let us possess one world, each hath one, and is one.

My face in thine eye, thine in mine appears,
And true plain hearts do in the faces rest,
Where can we find two better hemispheres
Without sharp north, without declining west?
Whatever dies, was not mixed equally;
If our two loves be one, or, thou and I
Love so alike, that none do slacken, none can die.

Song

Go, and catch a falling star,
    Get with child a mandrake root,
Tell me, where all past years are,
    Or who cleft the devil's foot,
Teach me to hear mermaids singing,
    Or to keep off envy's stinging,
        And find
        What wind
Serves to advance an honest mind.

If thou beest born to strange sights,
    Things invisible to see,
Ride ten thousand days and nights,
    Till age snow white hairs on thee,
Thou, when thou return'st, wilt tell me
All strange wonders that befell thee,
                And swear
                Nowhere
Lives a woman true, and fair.

If thou findst one, let me know,
    Such a pilgrimage were sweet;
Yet do not, I would not go,
    Though at next door we might meet,
Though she were true, when you met her,

And last, till you write your letter,
        Yet she
        Will be
False, ere I come, to two, or three.

Woman's Constancy

Now thou hast loved me one whole day,
Tomorrow when thou leav'st, what wilt thou say?
Wilt thou then antedate some new made vow?
        Or say that now
We are not just those persons, which we were?
Or, that oaths made in reverential fear
Of love, and his wrath, any may forswear?
Or, as true deaths, true marriages untie,
So lovers' contracts, images of those,
Bind but till sleep, death's image, them unloose?
        Or, your own end to justify,
For having purposed change, and falsehood, you
Can have no way but falsehood to be true?
Vain lunatic, against these 'scapes I could
        Dispute, and conquer, if I would,
        Which I abstain to do,
For by tomorrow, I may think so too.

The Undertaking

I have done one braver thing
    Than all the Worthies did,
And yet a braver thence doth spring,
    Which is, to keep that hid.

It were but madness now t'impart
    The skill of specular stone,
When he which can have learned the art
    To cut it, and find none.

So, if I now should utter this,
    Others (because no more
Such stuff to work upon, there is,)
    Would love but as before.

But he who loveliness within
    Hath found, all outward loathes,

For he who color loves, and skin,
  Loves but their oldest clothes.

If, as I have, you also do
  Virtue attired in woman see,
And dare love that, and say so too,
  And forget the he and she;

And if this love, though placed so,
  From profane men you hide,
Which will no faith on this bestow,
  Or, if they do, deride:

Then you have done a braver thing
  Than all the Worthies did;
And a braver thence will spring,
  Which is, to keep that hid.

The Sun Rising

  Busy old fool, unruly sun,
    Why dost thou thus,
Through windows, and through curtains call on us?
Must to thy motions lovers' seasons run?
    Saucy pedantic wretch, go chide
    Late schoolboys, and sour prentices,
  Go tell court-huntsmen, that the King will ride,
  Call country ants to harvest offices;
Love, all alike, no season knows, nor clime,
Nor hours, days, months, which are the rags of time.

    Thy beams, so reverend, and strong
      Why shouldst thou think?
I could eclipse and cloud them with a wink,
But that I would not lose her sight so long:
    If her eyes have not blinded thine,
    Look, and tomorrow late, tell me,
  Whether both the Indias of spice and mine
  Be where thou leftst them, or lie here with me.
Ask for those kings whom thou saw'st yesterday,
And thou shalt hear, all here in one bed lay.

    She is all states, and all princes, I,
      Nothing else is.
Princes do but play us; compared to this,
All honor's mimic; all wealth alchemy.

Thou sun art half as happy as we,
In that the world's contracted thus;
Thine age asks ease, and since thy duties be
To warm the world, that's done in warming us.
Shine here to us, and thou art everywhere;
This bed thy center is, these walls, thy sphere.

The Indifferent

I can love both fair and brown,
Her whom abundance melts, and her whom want betrays,
Her who loves loneness best, and her who masks and plays,
Her whom the country formed, and whom the town,
Her who believes, and her who tries,
Her who still weeps with spongy eyes,
And her who is dry cork, and never cries;
I can love her, and her, and you and you,
I can love any, so she be not true.

Will no other vice content you?
Will it not serve your turn to do, as did your mothers?
Or have you all old vices spent, and now would find out others?
Or doth a fear, that men are true, torment you?
Oh we are not, be not you so,
Let me, and do you, twenty know.
Rob me, but bind me not, and let me go.
Must I, who came to travel through you,
Grow your fixed subject, because you are true?

Venus heard me sigh this song,
And by love's sweetest part, variety, she swore,
She heard not this till now; and that it should be so no more.
She went, examined, and returned ere long,
And said, "Alas, some two or three
Poor heretics in love there be,
Which think to stablish dangerous constancy.
But I have told them, 'Since you will be true,
You shall be true to them, who are false to you.'"

The Canonization

For God's sake hold your tongue, and let me love,
Or chide my palsy, or my gout,
My five gray hairs, or ruined fortune flout,
With wealth your state, your mind with arts improve,

Take you a course, get you a place,
Observe his Honor, or his Grace,
Or the King's real, or his stamped face
Contemplate; what you will, approve,
So you will let me love.

Alas, alas, who's injured by my love?
What merchant's ships have my sighs drowned?
Who says my tears have overflowed his ground?
When did my colds a forward spring remove?
When did the heats which my veins fill
Add one more to the plaguy bill?
Soldiers find wars, and lawyers find out still
Litigious men, which quarrels move,
Though she and I do love.

Call us what you will, we are made such by love;
Call her one, me another fly,
We are tapers too, and at our own cost die,
And we in us find the eagle and the dove.
The phoenix riddle hath more wit
By us; we two being one, are it.
So to one neutral thing both sexes fit,
We die and rise the same, and prove
Mysterious by this love.

We can die by it, if not live by love,
And if unfit for tombs and hearse
Our legend be, it will be fit for verse;
And if no piece of chronicle we prove,
We'll build in sonnets pretty rooms;
As well a well wrought urn becomes
The greatest ashes, as half-acre tombs,
And by these hymns, all shall approve
Us canonized for love.

And thus invoke us: "You whom reverend love
Made one another's hermitage;
You, to whom love was peace, that now is rage;
Who did the whole world's soul contract, and drove
Into the glasses of your eyes
(So made such mirrors, and such spies,
That they did all to you epitomize)
Countries, towns, courts: beg from above
A pattern of your love!"

The Triple Fool

I am two fools, I know,
For loving, and for saying so
   In whining poetry;
But where's that wiseman, that would not be I,
   If she would not deny?
Then as th'earth's inward narrow crooked lanes
Do purge seawater's fretful salt away,
   I thought, if I could draw my pains
Through rhyme's vexation, I should them allay.
Grief brought to numbers cannot be so fierce,
For, he tames it, that fetters it in verse.

But when I have done so,
Some man, his art and voice to show,
   Doth set and sing my pain,
And, by delighting many, frees again
   Grief, which verse did restrain.
To love and grief tribute of verse belongs,
But not of such as pleases when 'tis read,
   Both are increased by such songs:
For both their triumphs so are published,
And I, which was two fools, do so grow three;
Who are a little wise, the best fools be.

Song

Sweetest love, I do not go,
   For weariness of thee,
Nor in hope the world can show
   A fitter love for me;
     But since that I
Must die at last, 'tis best,
To use myself in jest
   Thus by feigned deaths to die.

Yesternight the sun went hence,
   And yet is here today,
He hath no desire nor sense.
   Nor half so short a way:
     Then fear not me,
But believe that I shall make

Speedier journeys, since I take
   More wings and spurs than he.

O how feeble is man's power,
   That if good fortune fall,
Cannot add another hour,
   Nor a lost hour recall!
     But come bad chance,
And we join to it our strength,
And we teach it art and length,
   Itself o'er us to advance.

When thou sigh'st, thou sigh'st not wind,
   But sigh'st my soul away,
When thou weep'st, unkindly kind,
   My life's blood doth decay.
     It cannot be
That thou lov'st me, as thou say'st,
If in thine my life thou waste,
   That art the best of me.

Let not thy divining heart
   Forethink me any ill,
Destiny may take thy part,
   And may thy fears fulfill;
     But think that we
Are but turned aside to sleep;
They who one another keep
   Alive, ne'er parted be.

The Legacy

When I died last, and, dear, I die
  As often as from thee I go,
   Though it be but an hour ago,
And lovers' hours be full eternity,
I can remember yet, that I
  Something did say, and something did bestow;
Though I be dead, which sent me, I should be
Mine own executor and legacy.

I heard me say, Tell her anon,
  That myself (that is you, not I)
   Did kill me, and when I felt me die,
I bid me send my heart, when I was gone,

But I alas could there find none,
    When I had ripped me, and searched where hearts did lie;
It killed me again, that I who still was true,
In life, in my last will should cozen you.

Yet I found something like a heart,
    But colors it, and corners had,
    It was not good, it was not bad,
It was entire to none, and few had part.
As good as could be made by art
    It seemed; and therefore for our losses sad,
I meant to send this heart instead of mine,
But oh, no man could hold it, for 'twas thine.

A Fever

Oh do not die, for I shall hate
    All women so, when thou art gone,
That thee I shall not celebrate,
    When I remember, thou wast one.

But yet thou canst not die, I know;
    To leave this world behind, is death,
But when thou from this world wilt go,
    The whole world vapors with thy breath.

Or if, when thou, the world's soul, goest,
    It stay, 'tis but thy carcass then,
The fairest woman, but thy ghost,
    But corrupt worms, the worthiest men.

O wrangling schools, that search what fire
    Shall burn this world, had none the wit
Unto this knowledge to aspire,
    That this her fever might be it?

And yet she cannot waste by this,
    Nor long bear this torturing wrong,
For such corruption needful is
    To fuel such a fever long.

These burning fits but meteors be,
    Whose matter in thee is soon spent.
Thy beauty, and all parts, which are thee,
    Are unchangeable firmament.

Yet 'twas of my mind, seizing thee,
    Though it in thee cannot persever.
For I had rather owner be
    Of thee one hour, than all else ever.

Air and Angels

Twice or thrice had I loved thee,
Before I knew thy face or name;
So in a voice, so in a shapeless flame,
Angels affect us oft, and worshiped be;
    Still when, to where thou wert, I came,
Some lovely glorious nothing I did see.
    But since my soul, whose child love is,
Takes limbs of flesh, and else could nothing do,
    More subtle than the parent is,
Love must not be, but take a body too,
    And therefore what thou wert, and who,
        I bid love ask, and now
That it assume thy body, I allow,
And fix itself in thy lip, eye, and brow.

Whilst thus to ballast love, I thought,
And so more steadily to have gone,
With wares which would sink admiration,
I saw, I had love's pinnace overfraught,
    Every thy hair for love to work upon
Is much too much, some fitter must be sought;
    For, nor in nothing, nor in things
Extreme, and scatt'ring bright, can love inhere;
    Then as an angel, face and wings
Of air, not pure as it, yet pure doth wear,
    So thy love may be my love's sphere;
        Just such disparity
As is 'twixt air and angels' purity,
'Twixt women's love, and men's will ever be.

Break of Day

'Tis true, 'tis day; what though it be?
O wilt thou therefore rise from me?
Why should we rise, because 'tis light?
Did we lie down, because 'twas night?
Love which in spite of darkness brought us hither,
Should in despite of light keep us together.

Light hath no tongue, but is all eye;
If it could speak as well as spy,
This were the worst, that it could say,
That being well, I fain would stay,
And that I loved my heart and honor so,
That I would not from him, that had them, go.

Must business thee from hence remove?
Oh, that's the worst disease of love,
The poor, the foul, the false, love can
Admit, but not the busied man.
He which hath business, and makes love, doth do
Such wrong, as when a married man doth woo.

The Anniversary

All kings, and all their favorites,
    All glory of honors, beauties, wits,
The sun itself, which makes times, as they pass,
Is elder by a year, now, than it was
When thou and I first one another saw:
All other things, to their destruction draw,
    Only our love hath no decay;
This, no tomorrow hath, nor yesterday,
Running it never runs from us away,
But truly keeps his first, last, everlasting day.

Two graves must hide thine and my corse,
    If one might, death were no divorce.
Alas, as well as other princes, we
(Who prince enough in one another be)
Must leave at last in death, these eyes, and ears,
Oft fed with true oaths, and with sweet salt tears;
    But souls where nothing dwells but love
(All other thoughts being inmates) then shall prove
This, or a love increased there above,
When bodies to their graves, souls from their graves remove.

And then we shall be thoroughly blessed,
    But we no more, than all the rest;
Here upon earth, we are kings, and none but we
Can be such kings, nor of such subjects be.
Who is so safe as we? where none can do
Treason to us, except one of us two.
    True and false fears let us refrain,

Let us love nobly, and live, and add again
Years and years unto years, till we attain
To write threescore: this is the second of our reign.

A Valediction: of My Name, in the Window

My name engraved herein,
Doth contribute my firmness to this glass,
  Which, ever since that charm, hath been
  As hard, as that which graved it, was;
Thine eye will give it price enough, to mock
    The diamonds of either rock.

'Tis much that glass should be
As all confessing, and through-shine as I,
  'Tis more, that it shows thee to thee,
  And clear reflects thee to thine eye.
But all such rules, love's magic can undo,
    Here you see me, and I am you.

As no one point, nor dash,
Which are but accessories to this name,
  The showers and tempests can outwash,
  So shall all times find me the same;
You this entireness better may fulfill,
    Who have the pattern with you still.

Or if too hard and deep
This learning be, for a scratched name to teach,
  It, as a given death's-head keep,
  Lovers' mortality to preach,
Or think this ragged bony name to be
    My ruinous anatomy.

Then, as all my souls be
Emparadised in you (in whom alone
I understand, and grow and see),
  The rafters of my body, bone
Being still with you, the muscle, sinew, and vein,
    Which tile this house, will come again.

Till my return, repair
And recompact my scattered body so.
    As all the virtuous powers which are
    Fixed in the stars, are said to flow

Into such characters, as graved be
      When these stars have supremacy:

      So since this name was cut
When love and grief their exaltation had,
  No door 'gainst this name's influence shut;
  As much more loving, as more sad,
'Twill make thee; and thou shouldst, till I return,
      Since I die daily, daily mourn.

      When thy inconsiderate hand
Flings ope this casement, with my trembling name,
  To look on one, whose wit or land,
  New battery to thy heart may frame,
Then think this name alive, and that thou thus
      In it offendst my genius.

      And when thy melted maid,
Corrupted by thy lover's gold, and page,
  His letter at thy pillow hath laid,
  Disputed it, and tamed thy rage,
And thou begin'st to thaw towards him, for this,
      May my name step in, and hide his.

      And if this treason go
To an overt act, and that thou write again;
  In superscribing, this name flow
  Into thy fancy, from the pane.
So, in forgetting thou rememberest right,
      And unaware to me shalt write.

      But glass, and lines must be
No means our firm substantial love to keep;
  Near death inflicts this lethargy,
  And this I murmur in my sleep;
Impute this idle talk, to that I go,
      For dying men talk often so.

Twickenham Garden

Blasted with sighs, and surrounded with tears,
  Hither I come to seek the spring,
  And at mine eyes, and at mine ears,
Receive such balms, as else cure everything;
  But O, self-traitor, I do bring
The spider love, which transubstantiates all,

And can convert manna to gall,
And that this place may thoroughly be thought
    True paradise, I have the serpent brought.

'Twere wholesomer for me, that winter did
    Benight the glory of this place,
    And that a grave frost did forbid
These trees to laugh, and mock me to my face;
    But that I may not this disgrace
Endure, nor yet leave loving, Love, let me
    Some senseless piece of this place be;
Make me a mandrake, so I may groan here,
    Or a stone fountain weeping out my year.

Hither with crystal vials, lovers come,
    And take my tears, which are love's wine,
    And try your mistress' tears at home,
For all are false, that taste not just like mine;
    Alas, hearts do not in eyes shine,
Nor can you more judge woman's thoughts by tears,
    Than by her shadow, what she wears.
O perverse sex, where none is true but she,
    Who's therefore true, because her truth kills me.

A Valediction: of Weeping

        Let me pour forth
My tears before thy face, whilst I stay here,
For thy face coins them, and thy stamp they bear,
And by this mintage they are something worth,
        For thus they be
        Pregnant of thee;
Fruits of much grief they are, emblems of more,
When a tear falls, that thou falls which it bore,
So thou and I are nothing then, when on a divers shore.

        On a round ball
A workman that hath copies by, can lay
An Europe, Afric, and an Asia,
And quickly make that, which was nothing, all,
        So doth each tear,
        Which thee doth wear,
A globe, yea world by that impression grow,

Till thy tears mixed with mine do overflow
This world, by waters sent from thee, my heaven dissolved so.

      O more than moon,
Draw not up seas to drown me in thy sphere,
Weep me not dead, in thine arms, but forbear
To teach the sea, what it may do too soon;
        Let not the wind
        Example find,
To do me more harm, than it purposeth;
Since thou and I sigh one another's breath,
Whoe'er sighs most, is cruelest, and hastes the other's death.

The Flea

Mark but this flea, and mark in this,
How little that which thou deny'st me is;
It sucked me first, and now sucks thee,
And in this flea, our two bloods mingled be;
Thou know'st that this cannot be said
A sin, nor shame, nor loss of maidenhead,
    Yet this enjoys before it woo,
    And pampered swells with one blood made of two,
    And this, alas, is more than we would do.

Oh stay, three lives in one flea spare,
Where we almost, yea more than married are.
This flea is you and I, and this
Our marriage bed, and marriage temple is;
Though parents grudge, and you, we are met,
And cloistered in these living walls of jet.
    Though use make you apt to kill me,
    Let not to that, self-murder added be,
    And sacrilege, three sins in killing three.

Cruel and sudden, hast thou since
Purpled thy nail, in blood of innocence?
Wherein could this flea guilty be,
Except in that drop which it sucked from thee?
Yet thou triumph'st, and say'st that thou
Find'st not thyself, nor me the weaker now;
    'Tis true, then learn how false fears be;
    Just so much honor, when thou yield'st to me,
    Will waste, as this flea's death took life from thee.

The Curse

Whoever guesses, thinks, or dreams he knows
Who is my mistress, wither by this curse;
      His only, and only his purse
      May some dull heart to love dispose,
And she yield then to all that are his foes;
    May he be scorned by one, whom all else scorn,
    Forswear to others, what to her he hath sworn,
    With fear of missing, shame of getting, torn:

Madness his sorrow, gout his cramp, may he
Make, by but thinking, who hath made him such:
      And may he feel no touch
      Of conscience, but of fame, and be
Anguished, not that 'twas sin, but that 'twas she:
    In early and long scarceness may he rot,
    For land which had been his, if he had not
    Himself incestuously an heir begot:

May he dream treason, and believe, that he
Meant to perform it, and confess, and die,
      And no record tell why:
      His sons, which none of his may be,
Inherit nothing but his infamy:
    Or may he so long parasites have fed,
    That he would fain be theirs, whom he hath bred,
    And at the last be circumcised for bread:

The venom of all stepdames, gamesters' gall,
What tyrants, and their subjects interwish,
      What plants, mine, beasts, fowl, fish,
      Can contribute, all ill which all
Prophets, or poets spake; and all which shall
    Be annexed in schedules unto this by me,
    Fall on that man; for if it be a she
    Nature beforehand hath out-cursed me.

A Nocturnal upon St. Lucy's Day, Being the Shortest Day

'Tis the year's midnight, and it is the day's,
Lucy's, who scarce seven hours herself unmasks,
    The sun is spent, and now his flasks
    Send forth light squibs, no constant rays;
      The world's whole sap is sunk:

The general balm th'hydroptic earth hath drunk,
Whither, as to the bed's-feet, life is shrunk,
Dead and interred; yet all these seem to laugh,
Compared with me, who am their epitaph.

Study me then, you who shall lovers be
At the next world, that is, at the next spring:
   For I am every dead thing,
    In whom love wrought new alchemy.
      For his art did express
A quintessence even from nothingness,
From dull privations, and lean emptiness:
He ruined me, and I am rebegot
Of absence, darkness, death; things which are not.

All others, from all things, draw all that's good,
Life, soul, form, spirit, whence they being have;
   I, by love's limbeck, am the grave
    Of all, that's nothing. Oft a flood
      Have we two wept, and so
Drowned the whole world, us two; oft did we grow
To be two chaoses, when we did show
Care to aught else; and often absences
Withdrew our souls, and made us carcasses.

But I am by her death (which word wrongs her)
Of the first nothing, the elixir grown;
   Were I a man, that I were one,
    I needs must know; I should prefer,
      If I were any beast,
Some ends, some means; yea plants, yea stones detest,
And love; all, all some properties invest;
If I an ordinary nothing were,
As shadow, a light, and body must be here.

But I am none; nor will my sun renew.
You lovers, for whose sake, the lesser sun
   At this time to the Goat is run
    To fetch new lust, and give it you,
      Enjoy your summer all;
Since she enjoys her long night's festival,
Let me prepare towards her, and let me call
This hour her vigil, and her eve, since this
Both the year's, and the day's deep midnight is.

Witchcraft by a Picture

I fix mine eye on thine, and there
   Pity my picture burning in thine eye.
My picture drowned in a transparent tear,
    When I look lower I espy;
      Hadst thou the wicked skill
By pictures made and marred, to kill,
How many ways mightst thou perform thy will?

But now I have drunk thy sweet salt tears,
   And though thou pour more I'll depart;
My picture vanished, vanish fears,
    That I can be endamaged by that art;
      Though thou retain of me
One picture more, yet that will be,
Being in thine own heart, from all malice free.

The Bait

Come live with me, and be my love,
And we will some new pleasures prove
Of golden sands, and crystal brooks,
With silken lines, and silver hooks.

There will the river whispering run
Warmed by thy eyes, more than the sun.
And there the enamored fish will stay,
Begging themselves they may betray.

When thou wilt swim in that live bath,
Each fish, which every channel hath,
Will amorously to thee swim,
Gladder to catch thee, than thou him.

If thou, to be so seen, be'st loath,
By sun, or moon, thou darkenest both,
And if myself have leave to see,
I need not their light, having thee.

Let others freeze with angling reeds,
And cut their legs, with shells and weeds,
Or treacherously poor fish beset,
With strangling snare, or windowy net:

Let coarse bold hands, from slimy nest
The bedded fish in banks out-wrest,

Or curious traitors, sleavesilk flies
Bewitch poor fishes' wandering eyes.

For thee, thou needst no such deceit,
For thou thyself art thine own bait;
That fish, that is not catched thereby,
Alas, is wiser far than I.

The Apparition

When by thy scorn, O murd'ress, I am dead,
And that thou thinkst thee free
From all solicitation from me,
Then shall my ghost come to thy bed,
And thee, feigned vestal, in worse arms shall see;
Then thy sick taper will begin to wink,
And he, whose thou art then, being tired before,
Will, if thou stir, or pinch to wake him, think
        Thou call'st for more,
And in false sleep will from thee shrink,
And then poor aspen wretch, neglected thou
Bathed in a cold quicksilver sweat wilt lie
        A verier ghost than I;
What I will say, I will not tell thee now,
Lest that preserve thee; and since my love is spent,
I had rather thou shouldst painfully repent,
Than by my threat'nings rest still innocent.

The Broken Heart

He is stark mad, whoever says,
    That he hath been in love an hour,
Yet not that love so soon decays,
    But that it can ten in less space devour;
Who will believe me, if I swear
That I have had the plague a year?
    Who would not laugh at me, if I should say,
    I saw a flask of powder burn a day?

Ah, what a trifle is a heart,
    If once into love's hands it come!
All other griefs allow a part
    To other griefs, and ask themselves but some;

They come to us, but us love draws,
He swallows us, and never chaws:
   By him, as by chained shot, whole ranks do die,
   He is the tyrant pike, our hearts the fry.

If 'twere not so, what did become
   Of my heart, when I first saw thee?
I brought a heart into the room,
   But from the room, I carried none with me:
If it had gone to thee, I know
Mine would have taught thine heart to show
   More pity unto me: but love, alas,
   At one first blow did shiver it as glass.

Yet nothing can to nothing fall,
   Nor any place be empty quite,
Therefore I think my breast hath all
   Those pieces still, though they be not unite;
And now as broken glasses show
A hundred lesser faces, so
   My rags of heart can like, wish, and adore,
   But after one such love, can love no more.

A Valediction: Forbidding Mourning

   As virtuous men pass mildly away,
      And whisper to their souls, to go,
   Whilst some of their sad friends do say,
      The breath goes now, and some say, no:

   So let us melt, and make no noise,
      No tear-floods, nor sigh-tempests move,
   'Twere profanation of our joys
      To tell the laity our love.

   Moving of th'earth brings harms and fears,
      Men reckon what it did and meant,
   But trepidation of the spheres,
      Though greater far, is innocent.

   Dull sublunary lovers' love
      (Whose soul is sense) cannot admit
   Absence, because it doth remove
      Those things which elemented it.

But we by a love, so much refined,
  That ourselves know not what it is,
Interassured of the mind,
  Care less, eyes, lips, and hands to miss.

Our two souls therefore, which are one,
  Though I must go, endure not yet
A breach, but an expansion,
  Like gold to airy thinness beat.

If they be two, they are two so
  As stiff twin compasses are two,
Thy soul the fixed foot, makes no show
  To move, but doth, if th'other do.

And though it in the center sit,
  Yet when the other far doth roam,
It leans, and hearkens after it,
  And grows erect, as that comes home.

Such wilt thou be to me, who must
  Like th'other foot, obliquely run;
Thy firmness draws my circle just,
  And makes me end, where I begun.

The Ecstasy

Where, like a pillow on a bed,
  A pregnant bank swelled up, to rest
The violet's reclining head,
  Sat we two, one another's best.
Our hands were firmly cemented
  With a fast balm, which thence did spring,
Our eye-beams twisted, and did thread
  Our eyes, upon one double string;
So to'intergraft our hands, as yet
  Was all the means to make us one,
And pictures in our eyes to get
  Was all our propagation.
As 'twixt two equal armies, fate
  Suspends uncertain victory,
Our souls (which to advance their state,
  Were gone out) hung 'twixt her, and me.
And whilst our souls negotiate there,
  We like sepulchral statues lay;

All day, the same our postures were,
    And we said nothing, all the day.
If any, so by love refined,
    That he soul's language understood,
And by good love were grown all mind,
    Within convenient distance stood,
He (though he knew not which soul spake,
    Because both meant, both spake the same)
Might thence a new concoction take,
    And part far purer than he came.
This ecstasy doth unperplex
    (We said) and tell us what we love,
We see by this, it was not sex,
    We see, we saw not what did move:
But as all several souls contain
    Mixture of things, they know not what,
Love, these mixed souls, doth mix again,
    And makes both one, each this and that.
A single violet transplant,
    The strength, the color, and the size,
(All which before was poor, and scant)
    Redoubles still, and multiplies.
When love, with one another so
    Interinanimates two souls,
That abler soul, which thence doth flow,
    Defects of loneliness controls.
We then, who are this new soul, know,
    Of what we are composed, and made,
For, th'atomies of which we grow,
    Are souls, whom no change can invade.
But O alas, so long, so far
    Our bodies why do we forbear?
They are ours, though they are not we, we are
    The intelligences, they the spheres.
We owe them thanks, because they thus,
    Did us, to us, at first convey,
Yielded their forces, sense, to us,
    Nor are dross to us, but allay.
On man heaven's influence works not so,
    But that it first imprints the air,
So soul into the soul may flow,
    Though it to body first repair.
As our blood labors to beget

  Spirits, as like souls as it can,
Because such fingers need to knit
  That subtle knot, which makes us man:
So must pure lovers' souls descend
  T'affections, and to faculties,
Which sense may reach and apprehend,
  Else a great prince in prison lies.
To our bodies turn we then, that so
  Weak men on love revealed may look;
Love's mysteries in souls do grow,
  But yet the body is his book.
And if some lover, such as we,
  Have heard this dialogue of one,
Let him still mark us, he shall see
  Small change, when we are to bodies gone.

Love's Deity

I long to talk with some old lover's ghost,
  Who died before the god of love was born:
I cannot think that he, who then loved most,
  Sunk so low, as to love one which did scorn.
But since this god produced a destiny,
And that vice-nature, custom, lets it be;
  I must love her, that loves not me.

Sure, they which made him god, meant not so much,
  Nor he, in his young godhead practiced it.
But when an even flame two hearts did touch,
  His office was indulgently to fit
Actives to passives. Correspondency
Only his subject was. It cannot be
  Love, till I love her, that loves me.

But every modern god will now extend
  His vast prerogative, as far as Jove.
To rage, to lust, to write to, to commend,
  All is the purlieu of the god of love.
Oh were we wakened by this tyranny
To ungod this child again, it could not be
  I should love her, who loves not me.

Rebel and atheist too, why murmur I,
  As though I felt the worst that love could do?
Love might make me leave loving, or might try

    A deeper plague, to make her love me too,
    Which, since she loves before, I am loth to see;
    Falsehood is worse than hate; and that must be,
       If she whom I love, should love me.

The Funeral

Whoever comes to shroud me, do not harm
    Nor question much
That subtle wreath of hair, which crowns my arm;
The mystery, the sign you must not touch;
    For 'tis my outward soul,
Viceroy to that, which then to heaven being gone,
    Will leave this to control,
And keep these limbs, her provinces, from dissolution.

For if the sinewy thread my brain lets fall
    Through every part,
Can tie those parts, and make me one of all;
These hairs which upward grew, and strength and art
    Have from a better brain,
Can better do it; except she meant that I
    By this should know my pain,
As prisoners then are manacled, when they are condemned to die.

Whate'er she meant by it, bury it with me,
    For since I am
Love's martyr, it might breed idolatry,
If into others' hands these relics came;
    As 'twas humility
To afford to it all that a soul can do,
    So, 'tis some bravery,
That since you would save none of me, I bury some of you.

The Blossom

    Little think'st thou, poor flower,
      Whom I have watched six or seven days,
    And seen thy birth, and seen what every hour
    Gave to thy growth, thee to this height to raise,
    And now dost laugh and triumph on this bough,
      Little think'st thou
    That it will freeze anon, and that I shall
    Tomorrow find thee fall'n, or not at all.

Little think'st thou poor heart
   That labor'st yet to nestle thee,
And think'st by hovering here to get a part
In a forbidden or forbidding tree,
And hop'st her stiffness by long siege to bow:
      Little think'st thou,
That thou tomorrow, ere that sun doth wake,
Must with this sun, and me a journey take.

But thou which lov'st to be
   Subtle to plague thyself, wilt say,
Alas, if you must go, what's that to me?
Here lies my business, and here I will stay:
You go to friends, whose love and means present
      Various content
To your eyes, ears, and tongue, and every part.
If then your body go, what need you a heart?

Well then, stay here; but know,
   When thou hast stayed and done thy most;
A naked thinking heart, that makes no show,
Is to a woman, but a kind of ghost;
How shall she know my heart; or having none,
      Know thee for one?
Practice may make her know some other part,
But take my word, she doth not know a heart.

Meet me at London, then,
   Twenty days hence, and thou shalt see
Me fresher, and more fat, by being with men,
Than if I had stayed still with her and thee.
For God's sake, if you can, be you so too:
      I would give you
There, to another friend, whom we shall find
As glad to have my body, as my mind.

The Relic

When my grave is broke up again
Some second guest to entertain,
   (For graves have learned that woman-head
   To be to more than one a bed)
      And he that digs it, spies

A bracelet of bright hair about the bone,
        Will he not let us alone,
And think that there a loving couple lies,
Who thought that this device might be some way
To make their souls, at the last busy day,
Meet at this grave, and make a little stay?

        If this fall in a time, or land,
        Where mis-devotion doth command,
        Then, he that digs us up, will bring
        Us, to the Bishop, and the King,
            To make us relics; then
Thou shalt be a Mary Magdalen, and I
            A something else thereby;
All women shall adore us, and some men;
And since at such time, miracles are sought,
I would have that age by this paper taught
What miracles we harmless lovers wrought.

        First, we loved well and faithfully,
        Yet knew not what we loved, nor why,
        Difference of sex no more we knew,
        Than our guardian angels do;
            Coming and going, we
Perchance might kiss, but not between those meals;
            Our hands ne'er touched the seals,
Which nature, injured by late law, sets free:
These miracles we did; but now alas,
All measure, and all language, I should pass,
Should I tell what a miracle she was.

A Lecture upon the Shadow

Stand still, and I will read to thee
A lecture, love, in love's philosophy.
        These three hours that we have spent,
        Walking here, two shadows went
Along with us, which we ourselves produced;
But, now the sun is just above our head,
        We do those shadows tread;
        And to brave clearness all things are reduced.
    So whilst our infant loves did grow,
    Disguises did, and shadows, flow,
    From us, and our cares; but, now 'tis not so.

That love hath not attained the high'st degree,
Which is still diligent lest others see.

Except our loves at this noon stay,
We shall new shadows make the other way.
      As the first were made to blind
      Others; these which come behind
Will work upon ourselves, and blind our eyes.
If our loves faint, and westwardly decline;
      To me thou, falsely, thine,
      And I to thee mine actions shall disguise.
  The morning shadows wear away,
  But these grow longer all the day,
  But oh, love's day is short, if love decay.

Love is a growing, or full constant light;
And his first minute, after noon, is night.

A Burnt Ship

Out of a fired ship, which, by no way
But drowning, could be rescued from the flame,
Some men leaped forth, and ever as they came
Near the foes' ships, did by their shot decay;
So all were lost, which in the ship were found,
  They in the sea being burnt, they in the burnt ship drowned.

Fall of a Wall

Under an undermined, and shot-bruised wall
A too-bold captain perished by the fall,
Whose brave misfortune, happiest men envied,
That had a town for tomb, his bones to hide.

Elegy I: Jealousy

Fond woman, which wouldst have thy husband die,
And yet complain'st of his great jealousy;
If swoll'n with poison, he lay in his last bed,
His body with a sere-bark covered,
Drawing his breath, as thick and short, as can
The nimblest crocheting musician,
Ready with loathsome vomiting to spew
His soul out of one hell, into a new,
Made deaf with his poor kindred's howling cries,

Begging with few feigned tears, great legacies,
Thou wouldst not weep, but jolly, and frolic be,
As a slave, which tomorrow should be free;
Yet weep'st thou, when thou seest him hungerly
Swallow his own death, heart's-bane jealousy.
O give him many thanks, he is courteous,
That in suspecting kindly warneth us.
We must not, as we used, flout openly,
In scoffing riddles, his deformity;
Nor at his board together being sat,
With words, nor touch, scarce looks adulterate.
Nor when he swoll'n, and pampered with great fare
Sits down, and snorts, caged in his basket chair,
Must we usurp his own bed any more,
Nor kiss and play in his house, as before.
Now I see many dangers; for that is
His realm, his castle, and his diocese.
But if, as envious men, which would revile
Their prince, or coin his gold, themselves exile
Into another country, and do it there,
We play in another house, what should we fear?
There we will scorn his household policies,
His silly plots, and pensionary spies,
As the inhabitants of Thames' right side
Do London's Mayor; or Germans, the Pope's pride.

Elegy II: The Anagram

Marry, and love thy Flavia, for, she
Hath all things, whereby others beauteous be,
For, though her eyes be small, her mouth is great,
Though they be ivory, yet her teeth be jet,
Though they be dim, yet she is light enough,
And though her harsh hair fall, her skin is rough;
What though her cheeks be yellow, her hair's red,
Give her thine, and she hath a maidenhead.
These things are beauty's elements, where these
Meet in one, that one must, as perfect, please.
If red and white and each good quality
Be in thy wench, ne'er ask where it doth lie.
In buying things perfumed, we ask, if there
Be musk and amber in it, but not where.
Though all her parts be not in th'usual place,

She hath yet an anagram of a good face.
If we might put the letters but one way,
In the lean dearth of words, what could we say?
When by the gamut some musicians make
A perfect song, others will undertake,
By the same gamut changed, to equal it.
Things simply good, can never be unfit.
She's fair as any, if all be like her,
And if none be, then she is singular.
All love is wonder; if we justly do
Account her wonderful, why not lovely too?
Love built on beauty, soon as beauty, dies,
Choose this face, changed by no deformities.
Women are all like angels; the fair be
Like those which fell to worse; but such as thee,
Like to good angels, nothing can impair:
'Tis less grief to be foul, than to have been fair.
For one's night's revels, silk and gold we choose,
But, in long journeys, cloth, and leather use.
Beauty is barren oft; best husbands say,
There is best land, where there is foulest way.
Oh what a sovereign plaster will she be,
If thy past sins have taught thee jealousy!
Here needs no spies, nor eunuchs; her commit
Safe to thy foes; yea, to a marmoset.
When Belgia's cities, the round countries drown,
That dirty foulness guards, and arms the town:
So doth her face guard her; and so, for thee,
Which, forced by business, absent oft must be,
She, whose face, like clouds, turns the day to night,
Who, mightier than the sea, makes Moors seem white,
Who, though seven years, she in the stews had laid,
A nunnery durst receive, and think a maid,
And though in childbed's labor she did lie,
Midwives would swear, 'twere but a tympany,
Whom, if she accuse herself, I credit less
Than witches, which impossibles confess,
Whom dildoes, bedstaves, and her velvet glass
Would be as loth to touch as Joseph was:
One like none, and liked of none, fittest were,
For, things in fashion every man will wear.

Elegy V: His Picture

Here take my picture; though I bid farewell,
Thine, in my heart, where my soul dwells, shall dwell.
'Tis like me now, but I dead, 'twill be more
When we are shadows both, than 'twas before.
When weather-beaten I come back; my hand,
Perhaps with rude oars torn, or sunbeams tanned,
My face and breast of haircloth, and my head
With care's rash sudden storms, being o'erspread,
My body a sack of bones, broken within,
And powder's blue stains scattered on my skin;
If rival fools tax thee to have loved a man,
So foul, and coarse, as, oh, I may seem then,
This shall say what I was: and thou shalt say,
Do his hurts reach me? doth my worth decay?
Or do they reach his judging mind, that he
Should now love less, what he did love to see?
That which in him was fair and delicate,
Was but the milk, which in love's childish state
Did nurse it: who now is grown strong enough
To feed on that, which to disused tastes seems tough.

Elegy IX: The Autumnal

No spring, nor summer beauty hath such grace,
    As I have seen in one autumnal face.
Young beauties force our love, and that's a rape,
    This doth but counsel, yet you cannot 'scape.
If 'twere a shame to love, here 'twere no shame,
    Affection here takes reverence's name.
Were her first years the Golden Age; that's true,
    But now she's gold oft tried, and ever new.
That was her torrid and enflaming time,
    This is her tolerable tropic clime.
Fair eyes, who asks more heat than comes from hence,
    He in a fever wishes pestilence.
Call not these wrinkles, graves; if graves they were,
    They were love's graves; for else he is nowhere.
Yet lies not love dead here, but here doth sit
    Vowed to this trench, like an anachorit.*

---

*Anchorite.

And here, till hers, which must be his death, come,
   He doth not dig a grave, but build a tomb.
Here dwells he, though he sojourn everywhere,
   In progress, yet his standing house is here.
Here, where still evening is; not noon, nor night;
   Where no voluptuousness, yet all delight.
In all her words, unto all hearers fit,
   You may at revels, you at council, sit.
This is love's timber, youth his underwood;
   There he, as wine in June, enrages blood,
Which then comes seasonabliest, when our taste
   And appetite to other things, is past.
Xerxes' strange Lydian love, the platan tree,
   Was loved for age, none being so large as she,
Or else because, being young, nature did bless
   Her youth with age's glory, barrenness.
If we love things long sought, age is a thing
   Which we are fifty years in compassing.
If transitory things, which soon decay,
   Age must be loveliest at the latest day.
But name not winter-faces, whose skin's slack;
   Lank, as an unthrift's purse; but a soul's sack;
Whose eyes seek light within, for all here's shade;
   Whose mouths are holes, rather worn out, than made;
Whose every tooth to a several place is gone,
   To vex their souls at Resurrection;
Name not these living death's-heads unto me,
   For these, not ancient, but antique be.
I hate extremes; yet I had rather stay
   With tombs, than cradles, to wear out a day.
Since such love's natural lation* is, may still
   My love descend, and journey down the hill,
Not panting after growing beauties, so,
   I shall ebb out with them, who homeward go.

Elegy XVI: On His Mistress

   By our first strange and fatal interview,
   By all desires which thereof did ensue,
   By our long starving hopes, by that remorse
   Which my words' masculine persuasive force

---

*Movement.

Begot in thee, and by the memory
Of hurts, which spies and rivals threatened me,
I calmly beg: but by thy father's wrath,
By all pains, which want and divorcement hath,
I conjure thee, and all the oaths which I
And thou have sworn to seal joint constancy,
Here I unswear, and overswear them thus,
Thou shalt not love by ways so dangerous.
Temper, O fair love, love's impetuous rage,
Be my true mistress still, not my feigned page;
I'll go, and, by thy kind leave, leave behind
Thee, only worthy to nurse in my mind,
Thirst to come back; O if thou die before,
My soul from other lands to thee shall soar.
Thy (else almighty) beauty cannot move
Rage from the seas, nor thy love teach them love,
Nor tame wild Boreas' harshness; thou hast read
How roughly he in pieces shivered
Fair Orithea, whom he swore he loved.
Fall ill or good, 'tis madness to have proved
Dangers unurged; feed on this flattery,
That absent lovers one in th'other be.
Dissemble nothing, not a boy, nor change
Thy body's habit, nor mind's; be not strange
To thyself only; all will spy in thy face
A blushing womanly discovering grace;
Richly clothed apes are called apes, and as soon
Eclipsed as bright we call the moon the moon.
Men of France, changeable chameleons,
Spitals of diseases, shops of fashions,
Love's fuelers, and the rightest company
Of players, which upon the world's stage be,
Will quickly know thee, and no less, alas!
Th'indifferent Italian, as we pass
His warm land, well content to think thee page,
Will hunt thee with such lust, and hideous rage,
As Lot's fair guests were vexed. But none of these
Nor spongy hydroptic Dutch shall thee displease,
If thou here. O stay here, for, for thee
England is only a worthy gallery,
To walk in expectation, till from thence
Our greatest King call thee to his presence.
When I am gone, dream me some happiness,

Nor let thy looks our long hid love confess,
Nor praise, nor dispraise me, nor bless nor curse
Openly love's force, nor in bed fright thy nurse
With midnight's startings, crying out, "Oh, oh
Nurse, O my love is slain, I saw him go
O'er the white Alps alone; I saw him, I,
Assailed, fight, taken, stabbed, bleed, fall, and die."
Augur me better chance, except dread Jove
Think it enough for me to have had thy love.

Elegy XIX: To His Mistress Going to Bed

Come, Madam, come, all rest my powers defy,
Until I labor, I in labor lie.
The foe oft-times, having the foe in sight,
Is tired with standing though he never fight.
Off with that girdle, like heaven's zone glistering,
But a far fairer world encompassing.
Unpin that spangled breastplate which you wear,
That th'eyes of busy fools may be stopped there.
Unlace yourself, for that harmonious chime
Tells me from you, that now it is bedtime.
Off with that happy busk, which I envy,
That still can be, and still can stand so nigh.
Your gown going off, such beauteous state reveals,
As when from flowery meads th'hill's shadow steals.
Off with that wiry coronet and show
The hairy diadem which on you doth grow:
Now off with those shoes, and then safely tread
In this love's hallowed temple, this soft bed.
In such white robes, heaven's angels used to be
Received by men; thou angel bringst with thee
A heaven like Mahomet's paradise; and though
Ill spirits walk in white, we easily know,
By this these angels from an evil sprite,
Those set our hairs, but these our flesh upright.
   Licence my roving hands, and let them go,
Before, behind, between, above, below.
O my America! my new found land,
My kingdom, safeliest when with one man manned,
My mine of precious stones, my empery,
How blessed am I in this discovering thee!
To enter in these bonds, is to be free;

Then where my hand is set, my seal shall be.
    Full nakedness! All joys are due to thee;
As souls unbodied, bodies unclothed must be,
To taste whole joys. Gems which you women use
Are like Atlanta's balls, cast in men's views,
That when a fool's eye lighteth on a gem,
His earthly soul may covet theirs, not them.
Like pictures, or like books' gay coverings made
For laymen, are all women thus arrayed;
Themselves are mystic books, which only we
(Whom their imputed grace will dignify)
Must see revealed. Then since that I may know;
As liberally, as to a midwife, show
Thyself: cast all, yea, this white linen hence,
There is no penance due to innocence.
    To teach thee, I am naked first; why then
What needst thou have more covering than a man?

Satire I

Away thou fondling motley humorist,
Leave me, and in this standing wooden chest,
Consorted with these few books, let me lie
In prison, and here be coffined, when I die;
Here are God's conduits, grave divines; and here
Nature's secretary, the philosopher;
And jolly statesmen, which teach how to tie
The sinews of a city's mystic body;
Here gathering chroniclers, and by them stand
Giddy fantastic poets of each land.
Shall I leave all this constant company,
And follow headlong, wild uncertain thee?
First swear by thy best love in earnest
(If thou which lov'st all, canst love any best)
Thou wilt not leave me in the middle street,
Though some more spruce companion thou dost meet,
Not though a captain do come in thy way
Bright parcel gilt, with forty dead men's pay,
Not though a brisk perfumed pert courtier
Deign with a nod, thy courtesy to answer.
Nor come a velvet justice with a long
Great train of blue coats, twelve, or fourteen strong,
Wilt thou grin or fawn on him, or prepare

A speech to court his beauteous son and heir!
For better or worse take me, or leave me:
To take, and leave me is adultery.
Oh monstrous, superstitious Puritan,
Of refined manners, yet ceremonial man,
That when thou meet'st one, with inquiring eyes
Dost search, and like a needy broker prize
The silk, and gold he wears, and to that rate
So high or low, dost raise thy formal hat:
That wilt comfort none, until thou have known
What lands he hath in hope, or of his own,
As though all thy companions should make thee
Jointures, and marry thy dear company.
Why shouldst thou (that dost not only approve,
But in rank itchy lust, desire, and love
The nakedness and bareness to enjoy,
Of thy plump muddy whore, or prostitute boy)
Hate virtue, though she be naked, and bare?
At birth, and death, our bodies naked are;
And till our souls be unapparelled
Of bodies, they from bliss are banished.
Man's first blessed state was naked, when by sin
He lost that, yet he was clothed but in beast's skin,
And in this coarse attire, which I now wear,
With God, and with the Muses I confer.
But since thou like a contrite penitent,
Charitably warned of thy sins, dost repent
These vanities, and giddinesses, lo
I shut my chamber door, and come, let's go.
But sooner may a cheap whore, who hath been
Worn by as many several men in sin,
As are black feathers, or musk-color hose,
Name her child's right true father, 'mongst all those:
Sooner may one guess, who shall bear away
The Infanta of London, heir to an India;
And sooner may a gulling weather spy
By drawing forth heaven's scheme tell certainly
What fashioned hats, or ruffs, or suits next year
Our subtle-witted antic youths will wear;
Than thou, when thou depart'st from me, canst show
Whither, why, when, or with whom thou wouldst go.
But how shall I be pardoned my offence
That thus have sinned against my conscience?

Now we are in the street; he first of all
Improvidently proud, creeps tó the wall,
And so imprisoned, and hemmed in by me
Sells for a little state his liberty;
Yet though he cannot skip forth now to greet
Every fine silken painted fool we meet,
He them to him with amorous smiles allures,
And grins, smacks, shrugs, and such an itch endures,
As prentices, or schoolboys which do know
Of some gay sport abroad, yet dare not go.
And as fiddlers stop lowest, at highest sound,
So to the most brave, stoops he nigh'st the ground.
But to a grave man, he doth move no more
Than the wise politic horse would heretofore,
Or thou O elephant or ape wilt do,
When any names the King of Spain to you.
Now leaps he upright, jogs me, and cries, "Do you see
Yonder well-favored youth? Oh, 'tis he
That dances so divinely." "Oh," said I,
"Stand still, must you dance here for company?"
He drooped, we went, till one (which did excel
Th'Indians, in drinking his tobacco well)
Met us; they talked; I whispered, "Let us go,
'T may be you smell him not, truly I do."
He hears not me, but, on the other side
A many-colored peacock having spied,
Leaves him and me; I for my lost sheep stay;
He follows, overtakes, goes on the way,
Saying, "Him whom I last left, all repute
For his device, in handsoming a suit,
To judge of lace, pink, panes, print, cut, and pleat
Of all the Court to have the best conceit."
"Our dull comedians want him, let him go;
But oh, God strengthen thee, why stoop'st thou so?"
"Why? he hath traveled." "Long?" "No; but to me"
(Which understand none) "he doth seem to be
Perfect French, and Italian." I replied,
"So is the pox." He answered not, but spied
More men of sort, of parts, and qualities;
At last his love he in a window spies,
And like light dew exhaled, he flings from me
Violently ravished to his lechery.
Many were there, he could command no more;

He quarreled, fought, bled; and turned out of door
    Directly came to me hanging the head,
    And constantly a while must keep his bed.

Satire III

Kind pity chokes my spleen; brave scorn forbids
Those tears to issue which swell my eyelids;
I must not laugh, nor weep sins, and be wise,
Can railing then cure these worn maladies?
Is not our mistress fair religion,
As worthy of all our soul's devotion,
As virtue was to the first blinded age?
Are not heaven's joys as valiant to assuage
Lusts, as earth's honor was to them? Alas,
As we do them in means, shall they surpass
Us in the end, and shall thy father's spirit
Meet blind philosophers in heaven, whose merit
Of strict life may be imputed faith, and hear
Thee, whom he taught so easy ways and near
To follow, damned? O if thou dar'st, fear this;
This fear great courage, and high valor is.
Dar'st thou aid mutinous Dutch, and dar'st thou lay
Thee in ships' wooden sepulchers, a prey
To leaders' rage, to storms, to shot, to dearth?
Dar'st thou dive seas, and dungeons of the earth?
Hast thou courageous fire to thaw the ice
Of frozen north discoveries? and thrice
Colder than salamanders, like divine
Children in th'oven, fires of Spain, and the line,
Whose countries limbecks to our bodies be,
Canst thou for gain bear? and must every he
Which cries not, "Goddess," to thy mistress, draw,
Or eat thy poisonous words? courage of straw!
O desperate coward, wilt thou seem bold, and
To thy foes and his (who made thee to stand
Sentinel in his world's garrison) thus yield,
And for the forbidden wars, leave th'appointed field?
Know thy foes: the foul devil (whom thou
Strivest to please), for hate, not love, would allow
Thee fain, his whole realm to be quit; and as
The world's all parts wither away and pass,
So the world's self, thy other loved foe, is

In her decrepit wane, and thou loving this,
Dost love a withered and worn strumpet; last,
Flesh (itself's death) and joys which flesh can taste,
Thou lovest; and thy fair goodly soul, which doth
Give this flesh power to taste joy, thou dost loathe.
Seek true religion. O where? Mirreus
Thinking her unhoused here, and fled from us,
Seeks her at Rome; there, because he doth know
That she was there a thousand years ago,
He loves her rags so, as we here obey
The statecloth where the prince sat yesterday.
Crants to such brave loves will not be enthralled,
But loves her only, who at Geneva is called
Religion, plain, simple, sullen, young,
Contemptuous, yet unhandsome; as among
Lecherous humors, there is one that judges
No wenches wholesome, but coarse country drudges.
Graius stays still at home here, and because
Some preachers, vile ambitious bawds, and laws
Still new like fashions, bid him think that she
Which dwells with us, is only perfect, he
Embraceth her, whom his godfathers will
Tender to him, being tender, as wards still
Take such wives as their guardians offer, or
Pay values. Careless Phrygius doth abhor
All, because all cannot be good, as one
Knowing some women whores, dares marry none.
Gracchus loves all as one, and thinks that so
As women do in divers countries go
In divers habits, yet are still one kind,
So doth, so is religion; and this blind-
ness too much light breeds; but unmoved thou
Of force must one, and forced but one allow;
And the right; ask thy father which is she,
Let him ask his; though truth and falsehood be
Near twins, yet truth a little elder is;
Be busy to seek her, believe me this,
He's not of none, nor worst, that seeks the best.
To adore, or scorn an image, or protest,
May all be bad; doubt wisely; in strange way
To stand inquiring right, is not to stray;
To sleep, or run wrong, is. On a huge hill,
Cragged, and steep, truth stands, and he that will

Reach her, about must, and about must go;
And what the hill's suddenness resists, win so;
Yet strive so, that before age, death's twilight,
Thy soul rest, for none can work in that night.
To will, implies delay, therefore now do:
Hard deeds, the body's pains; hard knowledge too
The mind's endeavors reach, and mysteries
Are like the sun, dazzling, yet plain to all eyes.
Keep the truth which thou hast found; men do not stand
In so ill case here, that God hath with his hand
Signed kings blank-charters to kill whom they hate,
Nor are they vicars, but hangmen to fate.
Fool and wretch, wilt thou let thy soul be tied
To man's laws, by which she shall not be tried
At the last day? Oh, will it then boot thee
To say a Philip, or a Gregory,
A Harry, or a Martin taught thee this?
Is not this excuse for mere contraries,
Equally strong? cannot both sides say so?
That thou mayest rightly obey power, her bounds know;
Those past, her nature, and name is changed; to be
Then humble to her is idolatry.
As streams are, power is; those blessed flowers that dwell
At the rough stream's calm head, thrive and do well,
But having left their roots, and themselves given
To the stream's tyrannous rage, alas, are driven
Through mills, and rocks, and woods, and at last, almost
Consumed in going, in the sea are lost:
So perish souls, which more choose men's unjust
Power from God claimed, than God himself to trust.

To Mr. Rowland Woodward

Like one who in her third widowhood doth profess
Herself a nun, tied to retiredness,
So affects my Muse now, a chaste fallowness;

Since she to few, yet to too many hath shown
How love-song weeds, and satiric thorns are grown
Where seeds of better arts, were early sown.

Though to use, and love poetry, to me,
Betrothed to no one art, be no adultery;
Omissions of good, ill, as ill deeds be.

For though to us it seem, and be light and thin,
Yet in those faithful scales, where God throws in
Men's works, vanity weighs as much as sin.

If our souls have stained their first white, yet we
May clothe them with faith, and dear honesty,
Which God imputes, as native purity.

There is no virtue, but religion:
Wise, valiant, sober, just, are names, which none
Want, which want not vice-covering discretion.

Seek we then ourselves in ourselves; for as
Men force the sun with much more force to pass,
By gathering his beams with a crystal glass;

So we, if we into ourselves will turn,
Blowing our sparks of virtue, may outburn
The straw, which doth about our hearts sojourn.

You know, physicians, when they would infuse
Into any oil, the souls of simples, use
Places, where they may lie still warm, to choose.

So works retiredness in us; to roam
Giddily, and be everywhere, but at home,
Such freedom doth a banishment become.

We are but farmers of ourselves, yet may,
If we can stock ourselves, and thrive, uplay
Much, much dear treasure for the great rent day.

Manure thyself then, to thyself be approved,
And with vain outward things be no more moved,
But to know, that I love thee and would be loved.

To the Countess of Bedford on New Year's Day

This twilight of two years, not past nor next,
    Some emblem is of me, or I of this,
Who meteorlike, of stuff and form perplexed,
    Whose what, and where, in disputation is,
    If I should call me anything, should miss.

I sum the years, and me, and find me not
    Debtor to th'old, nor creditor to the new,
That cannot say, my thanks I have forgot,

Nor trust I this with hopes, and yet scarce true
This bravery is, since these times showed me you.

In recompense I would show future times
    What you were, and teach them to urge towards such.
Verse embalms virtue; and tombs, or thrones of rhymes,
    Preserve frail transitory fame, as much
    As spice doth bodies from corrupt air's touch.

Mine are short-lived; the tincture of your name
    Creates in them, but dissipates as fast,
New spirits: for, strong agents with the same
    Force that doth warm and cherish, us do waste;
    Kept hot with strong extracts, no bodies last:

So, my verse built of your just praise, might want
    Reason and likelihood, the firmest base,
And made of miracle, now faith is scant,
    Will vanish soon, and so possess no place,
    And you, and it, too much grace might disgrace.

When all (as truth commands assent) confess
    All truth of you, yet they will doubt how I,
One corn of one low anthill's dust, and less,
    Should name, know, or express a thing so high,
    And not an inch, measure infinity.

I cannot tell them, nor myself, nor you,
    But leave, lest truth be endangered by my praise,
And turn to God, who knows I think this true,
    And useth oft, when such a heart mis-says,
    To make it good, for, such a praiser prays.

He will best teach you, how you should lay out
    His stock of beauty, learning, favor, blood;
He will perplex security with doubt,
    And clear those doubts; hide from you, and show you good,
    And so increase your appetite and food;

He will teach you, that good and bad have not
    One latitude in cloisters, and in Court;
Indifferent there the greatest space hath got;
    Some pity is not good there, some vain disport,
    On this side sin, with that place may comport.

Yet he, as he bounds seas, will fix your hours,
    Which pleasure, and delight may not ingress,

And though what none else lost, be truliest yours,
    He will make you, what you did not, possess,
    By using others', not vice, but weakness.

He will make you speak truths, and credibly,
    And make you doubt, that others do not so:
He will provide you keys, and locks, to spy,
    And 'scape spies, to good ends, and he will show
    What you may not acknowledge, what not know.

For your own conscience, he gives innocence,
    But for your fame, a discreet wariness,
And though to 'scape, than to revenge offence
    Be better, he shows both, and to repress
    Joy, when your state swells, sadness when 'tis less.

From need of tears he will defend your soul,
    Or make a rebaptizing of one tear;
He cannot, (that's, he will not) disenrol
    Your name; and when with active joy we hear
    This private gospel, then 'tis our New Year.

Elegy on the Lady Markham

Man is the world, and death the ocean,
    To which God gives the lower parts of man.
This sea environs all, and though as yet
    God hath set marks, and bounds, 'twixt us and it,
Yet doth it roar, and gnaw, and still pretend,
    And breaks our banks, whene'er it takes a friend.
Then our land waters (tears of passion) vent;
    Our waters, then, above our firmament,
(Tears which our soul doth for her sins let fall)
    Take all a brackish taste, and funeral,
And even these tears, which should wash sin, are sin.
    We, after God's "No," drown our world again.
Nothing but man of all envenomed things
    Doth work upon itself, with inborn stings.
Tears are false spectacles, we cannot see
    Through passion's mist, what we are, or what she.
In her this sea of death hath made no breach,
    But as the tide doth wash the slimy beach,
And leaves embroidered works upon the sand,
    So is her flesh refined by death's cold hand.

As men of China, after an age's stay,
    Do take up porcelain, where they buried clay;
So at this grave, her limbeck, which refines
    The diamonds, rubies, sapphires, pearls, and mines,
Of which this flesh was, her soul shall inspire
    Flesh of such stuff, as God, when his last fire
Annuls this world, to recompense it, shall,
    Make and name then, th' elixir of this all.
They say, the sea, when it gains, loseth too;
    If carnal death (the younger brother) do
Usurp the body, our soul, which subject is
    To th' elder death, by sin, is freed by this;
They perish both, when they attempt the just;
    For, graves our trophies are, and both deaths' dust.
So, unobnoxious now, she hath buried both;
    For, none to death sins, that to sin is loth,
Nor do they die, which are not loth to die;
    So hath she this, and that virginity.
Grace was in her extremely diligent,
    That kept her from sin, yet made her repent.
Of what small spots pure white complains! Alas,
    How little poison cracks a crystal glass!
She sinned, but just enough to let us see
    That God's word must be true, all, sinners be.
So much did zeal her conscience rarefy,
    That, extreme truth lacked little of a lie,
Making omissions, acts; laying the touch
    Of sin, on things that sometimes may be such.
As Moses' cherubins, whose natures do
    Surpass all speed, by him are winged too:
So would her soul, already in heaven, seem then,
    To climb by tears, the common stairs of men.
How fit she was for God, I am content
    To speak, that death his vain haste may repent.
How fit for us, how even and how sweet,
    How good in all her titles, and how meet,
To have reformed this forward heresy,
    That women can no parts of friendship be;
How moral, how divine shall not be told,
    Lest they that hear her virtues, think her old:
And lest we take death's part, and make him glad
    Of such a prey, and to his triumph add.

La Corona

1

Deign at my hands this crown of prayer and praise,
Weaved in my low devout melancholy,
Though which of good, hast, yea art treasury,
All changing unchanged ancient of days;
But do not, with a vile crown of frail bays,
Reward my muse's white sincerity,
But what thy thorny crown gained, that give me,
A crown of glory, which doth flower always;
The ends crown our works, but thou crown'st our ends,
For, at our end begins our endless rest;
The first last end, now zealously possessed,
With a strong sober thirst, my soul attends.
'Tis time that heart and voice be lifted high,
Salvation to all that will is nigh.

2 ANNUNCIATION

Salvation to all that will is nigh;
That all, which always is all everywhere,
Which cannot sin, and yet all sins must bear,
Which cannot die, yet cannot choose but die,
Lo, faithful Virgin, yields himself to lie
In prison, in thy womb; and though he there
Can take no sin, nor thou give, yet he will wear
Taken from thence, flesh, which death's force may try.
Ere by the spheres time was created, thou
Wast in his mind, who is thy son, and brother;
Whom thou conceiv'st, conceived; yea thou art now
Thy maker's maker, and thy father's mother;
Thou hast light in dark; and shutst in little room,
Immensity cloistered in thy dear womb.

3 NATIVITY

Immensity cloistered in thy dear womb,
Now leaves his well-beloved imprisonment,
There he hath made himself to his intent
Weak enough, now into our world to come;
But oh, for thee, for him, hath th'inn no room?
Yet lay him in this stall, and from the Orient,

Stars, and wisemen will travel to prevent
Th'effect of Herod's jealous general doom.
Seest thou, my soul, with thy faith's eyes, how he
Which fills all place, yet none holds him, doth lie?
Was not his pity towards thee wondrous high,
That would have need to be pitied by thee?
Kiss him, and with him into Egypt go,
With his kind mother, who partakes thy woe.

a man of sorrows

Mary's partaking sorrow

4 TEMPLE

With his kind mother who partakes thy woe,
Joseph turn back; see where your child doth sit,
Blowing, yea blowing out those sparks of wit,
Which himself on the doctors did bestow;
The Word but lately could not speak, and lo
It suddenly speaks wonders, whence comes it,
That all which was, and all which should be writ,
A shallow seeming child, should deeply know?
His godhead was not soul to his manhood,
Nor had time mellowed him to this ripeness,
But as for one which hath a long task, 'tis good,
With the sun to begin his business,
He in his age's morning thus began
By miracles exceeding power of man.

5 CRUCIFYING

By miracles exceeding power of man,
He faith in some, envy in some begat,
For, what weak spirits admire, ambitious hate;
In both affections many to him ran,
But oh! the worst are most, they will and can,
Alas, and do, unto the immaculate,
Whose creature fate is, now prescribe a fate,
Measuring self-life's infinity to a span,
Nay to an inch. Lo, where condemned he
Bears his own cross, with pain, yet by and by
When it bears him, he must bear more and die.
Now thou art lifted up, draw me to thee,
And at thy death giving such liberal dole,
Moist, with one drop of thy blood, my dry soul.

6 RESURRECTION

Moist, with one drop of thy blood, my dry soul
Shall (though she now be in extreme degree
Too stony hard, and yet too fleshly) be
Freed by that drop, from being starved, hard, or foul,
And life, by this death abled, shall control
Death, whom thy death slew; nor shall to me
Fear of first or last death, bring misery,
If in thy little book my name thou enrol,
Flesh in that long sleep is not putrefied,
But made that there, of which, and for which 'twas;
Nor can by other means be glorified.
May then sin's sleep, and death's soon from me pass,
That waked from both, I again risen may
Salute the last, and everlasting day.

7 ASCENSION

Salute the last and everlasting day,
Joy at the uprising of this sun, and son,
Ye whose just tears, or tribulation
Have purely washed, or burnt your drossy clay;
Behold the Highest, parting hence away,
Lightens the dark clouds, which he treads upon,
Nor doth he by ascending, show alone,
But first he, and he first enters the way.
O strong ram, which hast battered heaven for me,
Mild lamb, which with thy blood, hast marked the path;
Bright torch, which shin'st, that I the way may see,
Oh, with thy own blood quench thy own just wrath,
And if thy holy Spirit, my Muse did raise,
Deign at my hands this crown of prayer and praise.

Holy Sonnets

I   Thou hast made me, and shall thy work decay?
     Repair me now, for now mine end doth haste,
     I run to death, and death meets me as fast,
     And all my pleasures are like yesterday;
     I dare not move my dim eyes any way,
     Despair behind, and death before doth cast
     Such terror, and my feeble flesh doth waste
     By sin in it, which it t'wards hell doth weigh;

Only thou art above, and when towards thee
By thy leave I can look, I rise again;
But our old subtle foe so tempteth me,   *The devil*
That not one hour myself I can sustain;
Thy grace may wing me to prevent his art,
And thou like adamant draw mine iron heart.

II As due by many titles I resign
Myself to thee, O God, first I was made
By thee, and for thee, and when I was decayed
Thy blood bought that, the which before was thine;
I am thy son, made with thyself to shine,
Thy servant, whose pains thou hast still repaid,
Thy sheep, thine image, and, till I betrayed
Myself, a temple of thy Spirit divine;
Why doth the devil then usurp on me?
Why doth he steal, nay ravish that's thy right?
Except thou rise and for thine own work fight,
Oh I shall soon despair, when I do see
That thou lov'st mankind well, yet wilt not choose me,
And Satan hates me, yet is loth to lose me.

III O might those sighs and tears return again
Into my breast and eyes, which I have spent,
That I might in this holy discontent
Mourn with some fruit, as I have mourned in vain;
In mine idolatry what showers of rain
Mine eyes did waste? what griefs my heart did rent?
That sufferance was my sin; now I repent;
'Cause I did suffer I must suffer pain.
Th'hydroptic drunkard, and night-scouting thief,
The itchy lecher, and self-tickling proud
Have the remembrance of past joys, for relief
Of coming ills. To (poor) me is allowed
No ease; for, long, yet vehement grief hath been
The effect and cause, the punishment and sin.

IV Oh my black soul! now thou art summoned
By sickness, death's herald, and champion;
Thou art like a pilgrim, which abroad hath done
Treason, and durst not turn to whence he is fled,
Or like a thief, which till death's doom be read,
Wisheth himself delivered from prison;
But damned and haled to execution,

Wisheth that still he might be imprisoned.
Yet grace, if thou repent, thou canst not lack;
But who shall give thee that grace to begin?
Oh make thyself with holy mourning black,
And red with blushing, as thou art with sin;
Or wash thee in Christ's blood, which hath this might
That being red, it dyes red souls to white.

V   I am a little world made cunningly
    Of elements, and an angelic sprite,
    But black sin hath betrayed to endless night
    My world's both parts, and (oh) both parts must die.
    You which beyond that heaven which was most high
    Have found new spheres, and of new lands can write,
    Pour new seas in mine eyes, that so I might
    Drown my world with my weeping earnestly,
    Or wash it if it must be drowned no more:
    But oh it must be burnt! alas the fire
    Of lust and envy have burnt it heretofore,
    And made it fouler; let their flames retire,
    And burn me O Lord, with a fiery zeal
    Of thee and thy house, which doth in eating heal.

VI This is my play's last scene, here heavens appoint
    My pilgrimage's last mile; and my race
    Idly, yet quickly run, hath this last pace,
    My span's last inch, my minute's latest point,
    And gluttonous death, will instantly unjoint
    My body, and soul, and I shall sleep a space,
    But my ever-waking part shall see that face,
    Whose fear already shakes my every joint:
    Then, as my soul, to heaven her first seat, takes flight,
    And earth-born body, in the earth shall dwell,
    So, fall my sins, that all may have their right,
    To where they are bred, and would press me, to hell.
    Impute me righteous, thus purged of evil,
    For thus I leave the world, the flesh, the devil.

VII At the round earth's imagined corners, blow
    Your trumpets, angels, and arise, arise
    From death, you numberless infinities
    Of souls, and to your scattered bodies go,
    All whom the flood did, and fire shall o'erthrow,
    All whom war, dearth, age, agues, tyrannies,

Despair, law, chance, hath slain, and you whose eyes,
Shall behold God, and never taste death's woe.
But let them sleep, Lord, and me mourn a space,
For, if above all these, my sins abound,
'Tis late to ask abundance of thy grace,
When we are there; here on this lowly ground,
Teach me how to repent; for that's as good
As if thou hadst sealed my pardon, with thy blood.

VIII   If faithful souls be alike glorified
As angels, then my father's soul doth see,
And adds this even to full felicity,
That valiantly I hell's wide mouth o'erstride:
But if our minds to these souls be descried
By circumstances, and by signs that be
Apparent in us, not immediately,
How shall my mind's white truth by them be tried?
They see idolatrous lovers weep and mourn,
And vile blasphemous conjurers to call
On Jesus' name, and pharisaical
Dissemblers feign devotion. Then turn
O pensive soul, to God, for he knows best
Thy true grief, for he put it in my breast.

IX   If poisonous minerals, and if that tree,
Whose fruit threw death on else immortal us,
If lecherous goats, if serpents envious
Cannot be damned, alas, why should I be?
Why should intent or reason, born in me,
Make sins, else equal, in me more heinous?
And mercy being easy, and glorious
To God, in his stern wrath, why threatens he?
But who am I, that dare dispute with thee
O God? Oh! of thine only worthy blood,
And my tears, make a heavenly Lethean flood,
And drown in it my sin's black memory;
That thou remember them, some claim as debt,
I think it mercy, if thou wilt forget.

X   Death be not proud, though some have called thee
Mighty and dreadful, for, thou art not so,
For, those, whom thou think'st, thou dost overthrow,
Die not, poor death, nor yet canst thou kill me.
From rest and sleep, which but thy pictures be,

Much pleasure, then from thee, much more must flow,
And soonest our best men with thee do go,
Rest of their bones, and soul's delivery.
Thou art slave to fate, chance, kings, and desperate men,
And dost with poison, war, and sickness dwell,
And poppy, or charms can make us sleep as well,
And better than thy stroke; why swell'st thou then?
One short sleep past, we wake eternally,
And death shall be no more; death, thou shalt die.

XI   Spit in my face you Jews, and pierce my side,
Buffet, and scoff, scourge, and crucify me,
For I have sinned, and sinned, and only he,
Who could do no iniquity, hath died:
But by my death cannot be satisfied
My sins, which pass the Jews' impiety:
They killed once an inglorious man, but I
Crucify him daily, being now glorified.
Oh let me then, his strange love still admire:
Kings pardon, but he bore our punishment.
And Jacob came clothed in vile harsh attire
But to supplant, and with gainful intent:
God clothed himself in vile man's flesh, that so
He might be weak enough to suffer woe.

XII   Why are we by all creatures waited on?
Why do the prodigal elements supply
Life and food to me, being more pure than I,
Simple, and further from corruption?
Why brook'st thou, ignorant horse, subjection?
Why dost thou bull, and boar so sillily
Dissemble weakness, and by one man's stroke die,
Whose whole kind, you might swallow and feed upon?
Weaker I am, woe is me, and worse than you,
You have not sinned, nor need be timorous.
But wonder at a greater wonder, for to us
Created nature doth these things subdue,
But their Creator, whom sin, nor nature tied,
For us, his creatures, and his foes, hath died.

XIII   What if this present were the world's last night?
Mark in my heart, O soul, where thou dost dwell,
The picture of Christ crucified, and tell
Whether that countenance can thee affright,

Tears in his eyes quench the amazing light,
Blood fills his frowns, which from his pierced head fell.
And can that tongue adjudge thee unto hell,
Which prayed forgiveness for his foes' fierce spite?
No, no; but as in my idolatry
I said to all my profane mistresses,
Beauty, of pity, foulness only is
A sign of rigor: so I say to thee,
To wicked spirits are horrid shapes assigned,
This beauteous form assures a piteous mind.

XIV   Batter my heart, three-personed God; for, you
As yet but knock, breathe, shine, and seek to mend;
That I may rise, and stand, o'erthrow me, and bend
Your force, to break, blow, burn and make me new.
I, like an usurped town, to another due,
Labor to admit you, but oh, to no end,
Reason your viceroy in me, me should defend,
But is captived, and proves weak or untrue.
Yet dearly I love you, and would be loved fain,
But am betrothed unto your enemy:
Divorce me, untie, or break that knot again,
Take me to you, imprison me, for I
Except you enthrall me, never shall be free,
Nor ever chaste, except you ravish me.

XV   Wilt thou love God, as he thee? then digest,
My soul, this wholesome meditation,
How God the Spirit, by angels waited on
In heaven, doth make his temple in thy breast.
The Father having begot a Son most blessed,
And still begetting, (for he ne'er begun)
Hath deigned to choose thee by adoption,
Coheir to his glory, and Sabbath's endless rest;
And as a robbed man, which by search doth find
His stol'n stuff sold, must lose or buy it again:
The Son of glory came down, and was slain,
Us whom he had made, and Satan stol'n, to unbind.
'Twas much, that man was made like God before,
But, that God should be made like man, much more.

XVI   Father, part of his double interest
Unto thy kingdom, thy Son gives to me,
His jointure in the knotty Trinity

He keeps, and gives to me his death's conquest.
This Lamb, whose death, with life the world hath blessed,
Was from the world's beginning slain, and he
Hath made two wills, which with the Legacy
Of his and thy kingdom, do thy sons invest.
Yet such are thy laws, that men argue yet
Whether a man those statutes can fulfill;
None doth; but all-healing grace and spirit
Revive again what law and letter kill.
Thy law's abridgment, and thy last command
Is all but love; oh let this last will stand!

XVII Since she whom I loved hath paid her last debt
To nature, and to hers, and my good is dead,
And her soul early into heaven ravished,
Wholly on heavenly things my mind is set.
Here the admiring her my mind did whet
To seek thee God; so streams do show their head;
But though I have found thee, and thou my thirst hast fed,
A holy thirsty dropsy melts me yet.
But why should I beg more love, when as thou
Dost woo my soul for hers; offering all thine:
And dost not only fear lest I allow
My love to saints and angels things divine,
But in thy tender jealousy dost doubt
Lest the world, flesh, yea devil put thee out.

XVIII Show me dear Christ, thy spouse, so bright and clear.
What! is it she, which on the other shore
Goes richly painted? or which robbed and tore
Laments and mourns in Germany and here?
Sleeps she a thousand, then peeps up one year?
Is she self truth and errs? now new, now outwore?
Doth she, and did she, and shall she evermore
On one, on seven, or on no hill appear?
Dwells she with us, or like adventuring knights
First travail we to seek and then make love?
Betray kind husband thy spouse to our sights,
And let mine amorous soul court thy mild dove,
Who is most true, and pleasing to thee, then
When she is embraced and open to most men.

XIX Oh, to vex me, contraries meet in one:
Inconstancy unnaturally hath begot

A constant habit; that when I would not
I change in vows, and in devotion
As humorous is my contrition
As my profane love, and as soon forgot:
As riddlingly distempered, cold and hot,
As praying, as mute; as infinite, as none.
I durst not view heaven yesterday; and today
In prayers, and flattering speeches I court God:
Tomorrow I quake with true fear of his rod.
So my devout fits come and go away
Like a fantastic ague: save that here
Those are my best days, when I shake with fear.

Good Friday, 1613. Riding Westward

Let man's soul be a sphere, and then, in this,
The intelligence that moves, devotion is,
And as the other spheres, by being grown
Subject to foreign motions, lose their own,
And being by others hurried every day,
Scarce in a year their natural form obey:
Pleasure or business, so, our souls admit
For their first mover, and are whirled by it.
Hence is't, that I am carried towards the west
This day, when my soul's form bends toward the east.
There I should see a sun, by rising set,
And by that setting endless day beget;
But that Christ on this Cross, did rise and fall,
Sin had eternally benighted all.
Yet dare I almost be glad, I do not see
That spectacle of too much weight for me.
Who sees God's face, that is self life, must die;
What a death were it then to see God die?
It made his own lieutenant Nature shrink,
It made his footstool crack, and the sun wink.
Could I behold those hands which span the poles,
And tune all spheres at once, pierced with those holes?
Could I behold that endless height which is
Zenith to us, and our antipodes,
Humbled below us? or that blood which is
The seat of all our souls, if not of his,
Made dirt of dust, or that flesh which was worn
By God, for his apparel, ragged, and torn?

If on these things I durst not look, durst I
Upon his miserable mother cast mine eye,
Who was God's partner here, and furnished thus
Half of that sacrifice, which ransomed us?
Though these things, as I ride, be from mine eye,
They are present yet unto my memory,
For that looks towards them; and thou look'st towards me,
O Savior, as thou hang'st upon the tree;
I turn my back to thee, but to receive
Corrections, till thy mercies bid thee leave.
O think me worth thine anger, punish me,
Burn off my rusts, and my deformity,
Restore thine image, so much, by thy grace,
That thou may'st know me, and I'll turn my face.

A Hymn to Christ, at the Author's Last Going into Germany

In what torn ship soever I embark,
That ship shall be my emblem of thy ark;
What sea soever swallow me, that flood
Shall be to me an emblem of thy blood;
Though thou with clouds of anger do disguise
Thy face; yet through that mask I know those eyes,
   Which, though they turn away sometimes,
      They never will despise.

I sacrifice this island unto thee,
And all whom I loved there, and who loved me;
When I have put our seas 'twixt them and me,
Put thou thy sea betwixt my sins and thee.
As the tree's sap doth seek the root below
In winter, in my winter now I go,
   Where none but thee, th'eternal root
      Of true love I may know.

Nor thou nor thy religion dost control,
The amorousness of an harmonious soul,
But thou would'st have that love thyself: as thou
Art jealous, Lord, so I am jealous now,
Thou lov'st not, till from loving more, thou free
My soul: whoever gives, take liberty:
   O, if thou car'st not whom I love
      Alas, thou lov'st not me.

Seal then this bill of my divorce to all,
On whom those fainter beams of love did fall;
Marry those loves, which in youth scattered be
On fame, wit, hopes (false mistresses) to thee.
Churches are best for prayer, that have least light:
To see God only, I go out of sight:
  And to 'scape stormy days, I choose
    An everlasting night.

Hymn to God My God, in My Sickness

Since I am coming to that holy room,
  Where, with thy choir of saints for evermore,
I shall be made thy music; as I come
  I tune the instrument here at the door,
  And what I must do then, think here before.

Whilst my physicians by their love are grown
  Cosmographers, and I their map, who lie
Flat on this bed, that by them may be shown
  That this is my southwest discovery
  Per fretum febris,[1] by these straits to die,

I joy, that in these straits, I see my west;
  For, though their currents yield return to none,
What shall my west hurt me? As west and east
  In all flat maps (and I am one) are one,
  So death doth touch the resurrection.

Is the Pacific Sea my home? Or are
  The eastern riches? Is Jerusalem?
Anyan, and Magellan, and Gibraltar,
  All straits, and none but straits, are ways to them,
  Whether where Japhet dwelt, or Cham, or Shem.

We think that Paradise and Calvary,
  Christ's Cross, and Adam's tree, stood in one place;
Look Lord, and find both Adams met in me;
  As the first Adam's sweat surrounds my face,
  May the last Adam's blood my soul embrace.

---

1 Through the strait of fever.

So, in his purple wrapped receive me Lord,
    By these his thorns give me his other crown;
And as to others' souls I preached thy word,
    Be this my text, my sermon to mine own,
        Therefore that he may raise the Lord throws down.

A Hymn to God the Father

Wilt thou forgive that sin where I begun,
    Which is my sin, though it were done before?
Wilt thou forgive those sins, through which I run,
    And do run still: though still I do deplore?
        When thou hast done, thou hast not done,
            For, I have more.

Wilt thou forgive that sin by which I have won
    Others to sin? and, made my sin their door?
Wilt thou forgive that sin which I did shun
    A year, or two: but wallowed in, a score?
        When thou hast done, thou hast not done,
            For I have more.

I have a sin of fear, that when I have spun
    My last thread, I shall perish on the shore;
Swear by thyself, that at my death thy sun
    Shall shine as he shines now, and heretofore;
        And, having done that, thou hast done,
            I fear no more.

ANDREW MARVELL (1621–1678)

Possessed of an extraordinarily subtle and introspective imagination, Andrew Marvell wrote lyrics of great beauty and charm, as well as panegyric and satiric poems dealing with public figures and affairs of state during one of England's most turbulent eras. Author of "To His Coy Mistress," one of the greatest of all metaphysical love poems, Marvell employed "pure and natural English" in composing his secular poems and devotional pieces. In many ways he is the ideal embodiment of the "metaphysical" poet. As Helen Gardner notes (*The Metaphysical Poets*, Penguin Books, 1985) his poems are "perfect exponents of all the 'metaphysical' qualities—passionate, paradoxical argument, touched with humour and learned imagery."

To His Coy Mistress

Had we but world enough, and time,
This coyness, lady, were no crime.
We would sit down, and think which way
To walk, and pass our long love's day.
Thou by the Indian Ganges' side
Should'st rubies find: I by the tide
Of Humber would complain. I would
Love you ten years before the Flood:
And you should if you please refuse
Till the conversion of the Jews.
My vegetable love should grow
Vaster than empires, and more slow.
An hundred years should go to praise
Thine eyes, and on thy forehead gaze.
Two hundred to adore each breast:
But thirty thousand to the rest.
An age at least to every part,
And the last age should show your heart.
For, lady, you deserve this state;
Nor would I love at lower rate.
   But at my back I always hear
Time's wingèd chariot hurrying near:
And yonder all before us lie
Deserts of vast eternity.
Thy beauty shall no more be found;
Nor, in thy marble vault, shall sound
My echoing Song: then worms shall try
That long preserv'd virginity:
And your quaint honor turn to dust,
And into ashes all my lust.
The grave's a fine and private place,
But none I think do there embrace.
   Now therefore, while the youthful hue
Sits on thy skin like morning dew,
And while thy willing soul transpires
At every pore with instant fires,
Now let us sport us while we may;
And now, like am'rous birds of prey,
Rather at once our time devour,
Than languish in his slow-chapp'd power

Let us roll all our strength, and all
Our sweetness, up into one ball:
And tear our pleasures with rough strife,
Thorough the iron gates of life.
Thus, though we cannot make our sun
Stand still, yet we will make him run.

The Definition of Love

My love is of a birth as rare
As 'tis for object strange and high:
It was begotten by Despair
Upon Impossibility.

Magnanimous Despair alone
Could show me so divine a thing,
Where feeble Hope could ne'er have flown
But vainly flapp'd its tinsel wing.

And yet I quickly might arrive
Where my extended soul is fix'd,
But Fate does iron wedges drive,
And always crowds itself betwixt.

For Fate with jealous eye does see
Two perfect loves; nor lets them close:
Their union would her ruin be,
And her tyrannic pow'r depose.

And therefore her decrees of steel
Us as the distant poles have plac'd,
(Though love's whole world on us doth wheel)
Not by themselves to be embrac'd,

Unless the giddy heaven fall,
And earth some new convulsion tear;
And, us to join, the world should all
Be cramp'd into a planisphere.

As lines so loves oblique may well
Themselves in every angle greet:
But ours so truly parallel,
Though infinite can never meet.

Therefore the love which us doth bind,
But Fate so enviously debars,
Is the conjunction of the mind,
And opposition of the stars.

The Mower to the Glowworms

Ye living lamps, by whose dear light
The nightingale does sit so late,
And studying all the summer-night,
Her matchless songs does meditate;

Ye country comets, that portend
No war, nor prince's funeral,
Shining unto no higher end
Than to presage the grass's fall;

Ye glowworms, whose officious flame
To wand'ring mowers shows the way,
That in the night have lost their aim,
And after foolish fires do stray;

Your courteous lights in vain you waste,
Since Juliana here is come,
For she my mind hath so displac'd
That I shall never find my home.

The Mower Against Gardens

Luxurious man, to bring his vice in use,
    Did after him the world seduce:
And from the fields the flow'rs and plants allure,
    Where Nature was most plain and pure.
He first enclos'd within the garden's square
    A dead and standing pool of air:
And a more luscious earth for them did knead,
    Which stupefi'd them while it fed.
The pink grew then as double as his mind;
    The nutriment did change the kind.
With strange perfumes he did the roses taint,
    And flowers themselves were taught to paint.
The tulip, white, did for complexion seek;
    And learn'd to interline its cheek:
Its onion root they then so high did hold,
    That one was for a meadow sold.
Another world was search'd, through oceans new,
    To find the marvel of Peru.
And yet these rarities might be allow'd,
    To man, that sov'reign thing and proud;
Had he not dealt between the bark and tree,
    Forbidden mixtures there to see.

No plant now knew the stock from which it came;
    He grafts upon the wild the tame:
That the uncertain and adult'rate fruit
    Might put the palate in dispute.
His green seraglio has its eunuchs too;
    Lest any tyrant him outdo.
And in the cherry he does Nature vex,
    To procreate without a sex.
'Tis all enforc'd; the fountain and the grot;
    While the sweet fields do lie forgot:
Where willing Nature does to all dispense
    A wild and fragrant innocence:
And fawns and fairies do the meadows till,
    More by their presence than their skill.
Their statues polish'd by some ancient hand,
    May to adorn the gardens stand:
But howsoe'er the figures do excel,
    The gods themselves with us do dwell.

Damon the Mower

    Hark how the mower Damon sung,
    With love of Juliana stung!
    While ev'rything did seem to paint
    The scene more fit for his complaint.
    Like her fair eyes the day was fair;
    But scorching like his am'rous care.
    Sharp like his scythe his sorrow was,
    And wither'd like his hopes the grass.

    "Oh what unusual heats are here,
     Which thus our sun-burn'd meadows sear!
     The grasshopper its pipe gives o'er;
     And hamstring'd frogs can dance no more.
     But in the brook the green frog wades;
     And grasshoppers seek out the shades.
     Only the snake, that kept within,
     Now glitters in its second skin.

    "This heat the sun could never raise,
     Nor Dog-star so inflames the days.
     It from an higher beauty grow'th,
     Which burns the fields and mower both:
     Which made the Dog, and makes the sun

Hotter than his own Phaeton.
Not July causeth these extremes,
But Juliana's scorching beams.

"Tell me where I may pass the fires
Of the hot day, or hot desires.
To what cool cave shall I descend,
Or to what gelid fountain bend?
Alas! I look for ease in vain,
When remedies themselves complain.
No moisture but my tears do rest,
Nor cold but in her icy breast.

"How long wilt thou, fair Shepherdess,
Esteem me, and my presents less?
To thee the harmless snake I bring,
Disarmèd of its teeth and sting.
To thee chameleons changing hue,
And oak leaves tipp'd with honey dew.
Yet thou ungrateful hast not sought
Nor what they are, nor who them brought.

"I am the Mower Damon, known
Through all the meadows I have mown.
On me the morn her dew distills
Before her darling daffodils.
And, if at noon my toil me heat,
The sun himself licks off my sweat.
While, going home, the ev'ning sweet
In cowslip-water bathes my feet.

"What, though the piping shepherd stock
The plains with an unnumber'd flock,
This scythe of mine discovers wide
More ground than all his sheep do hide.
With this the golden fleece I shear
Of all these closes ev'ry year.
And though in wool more poor than they,
Yet am I richer far in hay.

"Nor am I so deform'd to sight,
If in my scythe I lookèd right;
In which I see my picture done,
As in a crescent moon the sun.
The deathless fairies take me oft

To lead them in their dances soft;
And, when I tune myself to sing,
About me they contract their ring.

"How happy might I still have mow'd,
Had not Love here his thistles sow'd!
But now I all the day complain,
Joining my labor to my pain;
And with my scythe cut down the grass,
Yet still my grief is where it was:
But, when the iron blunter grows,
Sighing I whet my scythe and woes."

While thus he threw his elbow round,
Depopulating all the ground,
And, with his whistling scythe, does cut
Each stroke between the earth and root,
The edged steel by careless chance
Did into his own ankle glance;
And there among the grass fell down,
By his own scythe, the mower mown.

"Alas!" said he, "these hurts are slight
To those that die by Love's despite.
With shepherd's purse, and clown's allheal,
The blood I staunch, and wound I seal.
Only for him no cure is found,
Whom Juliana's eyes do wound.
'Tis death alone that this must do:
For, Death, thou art a mower too."

The Mower's Song

My mind was once the true survey
Of all these meadows fresh and gay;
And in the greenness of the grass
Did see its hopes as in a glass;
When Juliana came, and she
What I do to the grass, does to my thoughts and me.

But these, while I with sorrow pine,
Grew more luxuriant still and fine;
That not one blade of grass you spi'd,
But had a flower on either side;
When Juliana came, and she
What I do to the grass, does to my thoughts and me.

Unthankful meadows, could you so
A fellowship so true forgo,
And in your gaudy May-games meet,
While I lay trodden under feet?
When Juliana came, and she
What I do to the grass, does to my thoughts and me.

But what you in compassion ought,
Shall now by my revenge be wrought:
And flow'rs, and grass, and I and all,
Will in one common ruin fall.
For Juliana comes, and she
What I do to the grass, does to my thoughts and me.

And thus, ye meadows, which have been
Companions of my thoughts more green,
Shall now the heraldry become
With which I shall adorn my tomb;
For Juliana comes, and she
What I do to the grass, does to my thoughts and me.

The Unfortunate Lover

Alas, how pleasant are their days
With whom the infant Love yet plays!
Sorted by pairs, they still are seen
By fountains cool, and shadows green.
But soon these flames do lose their light,
Like meteors of a summer's night:
Nor can they to that region climb,
To make impression upon time.

'Twas in a shipwreck, when the seas
Rul'd, and the winds did what they please,
That my poor lover floating lay,
And, ere brought forth, was cast away:
Till at the last the master-wave
Upon the rock his mother drave;
And there she split against the stone,
In a Caesarean section.

The sea him lent these bitter tears
Which at his eyes he always bears.
And from the winds the sighs he bore,
Which through his surging breast do roar.

No day he saw but that which breaks
Through frighted clouds in forked streaks.
While round the rattling thunder hurl'd,
As at the fun'ral of the world.

While Nature to his birth presents
This masque of quarreling elements,
A num'rous fleet of corm'rants black,
That sail'd insulting o'er the wrack,
Receiv'd into their cruel care
Th' unfortunate and abject heir:
Guardians most fit to entertain
The orphan of the hurricane.

They fed him up with hopes and air,
Which soon digested to despair.
And as one corm'rant fed him, still
Another on his heart did bill.
Thus while they famish him, and feast,
He both consumèd, and increas'd:
And languishèd with doubtful breath,
Th' amphibium of life and death.

And now, when angry heaven would
Behold a spectacle of blood,
Fortune and he are call'd to play
At sharp before it all the day:
And tyrant Love his breast does ply
With all his wing'd artillery,
Whilst he, betwixt the flames and waves,
Like Ajax, the mad tempest braves.

See how he nak'd and fierce does stand,
Cuffing the thunder with one hand;
While with the other he does lock
And grapple with the stubborn rock:
From which he with each wave rebounds,
Torn into flames, and ragg'd with wounds.
And all he says, a lover drest
In his own blood does relish best.

This is the only banneret
That ever Love created yet:
Who though, by the malignant stars,

Forcèd to live in storms and wars:
Yet dying leaves a perfume here,
And music within every ear:
And he in story only rules,
In a field sable a lover gules.

The Gallery

Clora, come view my soul, and tell
Whether I have contriv'd it well.
Now all its several lodgings lie
Compos'd into one gallery;
And the great arras-hangings, made
Of various faces, by are laid;
That, for all furniture, you'll find
Only your picture in my mind.

Here thou art painted in the dress
Of an inhuman murderess,
Examining upon our hearts
Thy fertile shop of cruel arts:
Engines more keen than ever yet
Adornèd tyrant's cabinet,
Of which the most tormenting are
Black eyes, red lips, and curlèd hair.

But, on the other side, th' art drawn
Like to Aurora in the dawn;
When in the east she slumb'ring lies,
And stretches out her milky thighs;
While all the morning choir does sing,
And manna falls, and roses spring;
And, at thy feet, the wooing doves
Sit perfecting their harmless loves.

Like an enchantress here thou show'st,
Vexing thy restless lover's ghost;
And, by a light obscure, dost rave
Over his entrails, in the cave;
Divining thence, with horrid care,
How long thou shalt continue fair;
And (when inform'd) them throw'st away,
To be the greedy vulture's prey.

But, against that, thou sitt'st afloat
Like Venus in her pearly boat.
The halcyons, calming all that's nigh,
Betwixt the air and water fly.
Or, if some rolling wave appears,
A mass of ambergris it bears.
Nor blows more wind than what may well
Convoy the perfume to the smell.

These pictures and a thousand more,
Of thee, my gallery do store;
In all the forms thou canst invent
Either to please me, or torment:
For thou alone to people me,
Art grown a num'rous colony;
And a collection choicer far
Than or Whitehall's, or Mantua's were.

But, of these pictures and the rest,
That at the entrance likes me best:
Where the same posture, and the look
Remains, with which I first was took.
A tender shepherdess, whose hair
Hangs loosely playing in the air,
Transplanting flow'rs from the green hill,
To crown her head, and bosom fill.

The Fair Singer

To make a final conquest of all me,
Love did compose so sweet an enemy,
In whom both beauties to my death agree,
Joining themselves in fatal harmony;
That while she with her eyes my heart does bind,
She with her voice might captivate my mind.

I could have fled from one but singly fair:
My disentangled soul itself might save,
Breaking the curlèd trammels of her hair.
But how should I avoid to be her slave,
Whose subtle art invisibly can wreathe
My fetters of the very air I breathe?

It had been easy fighting in some plain,
Where victory might hang in equal choice,
But all resistance against her is vain,

Who has th' advantage both of eyes and voice,
And all my forces needs must be undone,
She having gainèd both the wind and sun.

Mourning

You, that decipher out the fate
Of human offsprings from the skies,
What mean these infants which of late
Spring from the stars of Chlora's eyes?

Her eyes confus'd, and doublèd o'er,
With tears suspended ere they flow;
Seem bending upwards, to restore
To heaven, whence it came, their woe.

When, molding of the wat'ry spheres,
Slow drops untie themselves away;
As if she, with those precious tears,
Would strow the ground where Strephon lay.

Yet some affirm, pretending art,
Her eyes have so her bosom drown'd,
Only to soften near her heart
A place to fix another wound.

And, while vain pomp does her restrain
Within her solitary bow'r,
She courts herself in am'rous rain,
Herself both Danaë and the show'r.

Nay others, bolder, hence esteem
Joy now so much her master grown,
That whatsoever does but seem
Like grief is from her windows thrown.

Nor that she pays, while she survives,
To her dead love this tribute due;
But casts abroad these donatives,
At the installing of a new.

How wide they dream! The Indian slaves
That sink for pearl through seas profound,
Would find her tears yet deeper waves
And not of one the bottom sound.

I yet my silent judgment keep,
Disputing not what they believe
But sure as oft as women weep,
It is to be suppos'd they grieve.

Ametas and Thestylis
Making Hay-Ropes

AMETAS
Think'st thou that this love can stand,
Whilst thou still dost say me nay?
Love unpaid does soon disband:
Love binds love as hay binds hay.

THESTYLIS
Think'st thou that this rope would twine
If we both should turn one way?
Where both parties so combine,
Neither love will twist nor hay.

AMETAS
Thus you vain excuses find,
Which yourself and us delay:
And love ties a woman's mind
Looser than with ropes of hay.

THESTYLIS
What you cannot constant hope
Must be taken as you may.

AMETAS
Then let's both lay by our rope,
And go kiss within the hay.

The Nymph Complaining for
the Death of Her Fawn

The wanton troopers riding by
Have shot my fawn and it will die.
Ungentle men! They cannot thrive
To kill thee. Thou ne'er didst alive

Them any harm: alas, nor could
Thy death yet do them any good.
I'm sure I never wish'd them ill;
Nor do I for all this; nor will:
But, if my simple pray'rs may yet

Prevail with heaven to forget
Thy murder, I will join my tears
Rather than fail. But, O my fears!
It cannot die so. Heaven's King
Keeps register of everything:
And nothing may we use in vain.
Ev'n beasts must be with justice slain;
Else men are made their deodands*
Though they should wash their guilty hands
In his warm life-blood, which doth part
From thine, and wound me to the heart,
Yet could they not be clean: their stain
Is dy'd in such a purple grain.
There is not such another in
The world, to offer for their sin.
    Unconstant Sylvio, when yet
I had not found him counterfeit,
One morning (I remember well)
Ti'd in this silver chain and bell,
Gave it to me: nay, and I know
What he said then; I'm sure I do.
Said he, look how your huntsman here
Hath taught a fawn to hunt his dear.
But Sylvio soon had me beguil'd.
This waxèd tame, while he grew wild,
And quite regardless of my smart,
Left me his fawn, but took his heart.
    Thenceforth I set myself to play
My solitary time away,
With this: and very well content,
Could so mine idle life have spent.
For it was full of sport; and light
Of foot and heart; and did invite
Me to its game: it seem'd to bless

---

*deodands: in English law, animals or objects having caused a death and forfeited to the
  Crown for pious uses.

Itself in me. How could I less
Than love it? O I cannot be
Unkind, t' a beast that loveth me.

   Had it liv'd long, I do not know
Whether it too might have done so
As Sylvio did: his gifts might be
Perhaps as false or more than he.
But I am sure, for ought that I
Could in so short a time espy,
Thy love was far more better than
The love of false and cruel men.

   With sweetest milk, and sugar, first
I it at mine own fingers nurs'd.
And as it grew, so every day
It wax'd more white and sweet than they.
It had so sweet a breath! And oft
I blush'd to see its foot more soft,
And white (shall I say than my hand?),
Nay, any lady's of the land.

   It is a wond'rous thing, how fleet
'Twas on those little silver feet.
With what a pretty skipping grace
It oft would challenge me the race:
And when 't had left me far away,
'Twould stay, and run again, and stay.
For it was nimbler much than hinds;
And trod, as on the four winds.

   I have a garden of my own,
But so with roses overgrown,
And lilies, that you would it guess
To be a little wilderness.
And all the springtime of the year
It only lovèd to be there.
Among the beds of lilies, I
Have sought it oft, where it should lie;
Yet could not, till itself would rise,
Find it, although before mine eyes.
For, in the flaxen lilies' shade,
It like a bank of lilies laid.
Upon the roses it would feed,
Until its lips ev'n seem'd to bleed:
And then to me 'twould boldly trip,
And print those roses on my lip.

But all its chief delight was still
On roses thus itself to fill:
And its pure virgin limbs to fold
In whitest sheets of lilies cold.
Had it liv'd long, it would have been
Lilies without, roses within.

    O help! O help! I see it faint:
And die as calmly as a saint.
See how it weeps. The tears do come
Sad, slowly dropping like a gum.
So weeps the wounded balsam: so
The holy frankincense doth flow.
The brotherless Heliades
Melt in such amber tears as these.

    I in a golden vial will
Keep these two crystal tears, and fill
It till it do o'erflow with mine;
Then place it in Diana's shrine.

    Now my sweet fawn is vanish'd to
Whither the swans and turtles go:
In fair Elysium to endure,
With milk-white lambs, and ermines pure.
O do not run too fast: for I
Will but bespeak thy grave, and die.

    First my unhappy statue shall
Be cut in marble; and withal,
Let it be weeping too: but there
Th' engraver sure his art may spare;
For I so truly thee bemoan,
That I shall weep though I be stone:
Until my tears, still dropping, wear
My breast, themselves engraving there.
There at my feet shalt thou be laid,
Of purest alabaster made:
For I would have thine image be
White as I can, though not as thee.

Daphnis and Chloe

Daphnis must from Chloe part:
Now is come the dismal hour
That must all his hopes devour,
All his labor, all his art.

Nature, her own sex's foe,
Long had taught her to be coy:
But she neither knew t' enjoy,
Nor yet let her lover go.

But, with this sad news surpris'd,
Soon she let that niceness fall;
And would gladly yield to all,
So it had his stay compris'd.

Nature so herself does use
To lay by her wonted state,
Lest the world should separate;
Sudden parting closer glues.

He, well read in all the ways
By which men their siege maintain,
Knew not that the fort to gain
Better 'twas the siege to raise.

But he came so full possess'd
With the grief of parting thence,
That he had not so much sense
As to see he might be bless'd.

Till Love in her language breath'd
Words she never spake before;
But then legacies no more
To a dying man bequeath'd.

For, alas, the time was spent,
Now the latest minute's run
When poor Daphnis is undone,
Between joy and sorrow rent.

At that *Why*, that *Stay my Dear*,
His disorder'd locks he tare;
And with rolling eyes did glare,
And his cruel fate forswear.

As the soul of one scarce dead,
With the shrieks of friends aghast,
Looks distracted back in haste,
And then straight again is fled;

So did wretched Daphnis look,
Frighting her he lovèd most.

At the last, this lover's ghost
Thus his leave resolvèd took.

"Are my hell and heaven join'd
 More to torture him that dies?
 Could departure not suffice,
 But that you must then grow kind?

"Ah, my Chloe, how have I
 Such a wretched minute found,
 When thy favors should me wound
 More than all thy cruelty?

"So to the condemnèd wight
 The delicious cup we fill;
 And allow him all he will,
 For his last and short delight.

"But I will not now begin
 Such a debt unto my foe;
 Nor to my departure owe
 What my presence could not win.

"Absence is too much alone:
 Better 'tis to go in peace,
 Than my losses to increase
 By a late fruition.

"Why should I enrich my fate?
 'Tis a vanity to wear,
 For my executioner,
 Jewels of so high a rate.

"Rather I away will pine
 In a manly stubbornness
 Than be fatted up express
 For the cannibal to dine.

"Whilst this grief does thee disarm,
 All th' enjoyment of our love
 But the ravishment would prove
 Of a body dead while warm.

"And I parting should appear
 Like the gourmand Hebrew dead,
 While with quails and Manna fed,
 He does through the desert err.

"Or the witch that midnight wakes
For the fern, whose magic weed
In one minute casts the seed,
And invisible him makes.

"Gentler times for love are meant;
Who for parting pleasure strain
Gather roses in the rain,
Wet themselves and spoil their scent.

"Farewell therefore all the fruit
Which I could from love receive:
Joy will not with sorrow weave,
Nor will I this grief pollute.

"Fate I come, as dark, as sad,
As thy malice could desire;
Yet bring with me all the fire
That love in his torches had."

At these words away he broke;
As who long has praying li'n,
To his headsman makes the sign,
And receives the parting stroke.

But hence virgins all beware.
Last night he with Phlogis slept;
This night for Dorinda kept;
And but rid to take the air.

Yet he does himself excuse;
Nor indeed without a cause.
For, according to the laws,
Why did Chloe once refuse?

The Match

Nature had long a treasure made
    Of all her choicest store;
Fearing, when she should be decay'd,
    To beg in vain for more.

Her orientest colors there,
    And essences most pure,
With sweetest perfumes hoarded were,
    All as she thought secure.

She seldom them unlock'd, or us'd,
   But with the nicest care;
For, with one grain of them diffus'd,
   She could the world repair.

But likeness soon together drew
   What she did separate lay;
Of which one perfect beauty grew,
   And that was Celia.

Love wisely had of long foreseen
   That he must once grow old;
And therefore stor'd a magazine,
   To save him from the cold.

He kept the several cells replete
   With nitre thrice refin'd;
The naphta's and the sulphur's heat,
   And all that burns the mind.

He fortif'd the double gate,
   And rarely thither came;
For, with one spark of these, he straight
   All nature could inflame.

Till, by vicinity so long,
   A nearer way they sought;
And, grown magnetically strong,
   Into each other wrought.

Thus all his fuel did unite
   To make one fire high:
None ever burn'd so hot, so bright;
   And, Celia, that am I.

So we alone the happy rest,
   Whilst all the world is poor,
And have within ourselves possess'd
   All love's and nature's store.

Young Love

Come, little infant, love me now,
   While thine unsuspected years
Clear thine agèd father's brow
   From cold jealousy and fears.

Pretty surely 'twere to see
    By young love old time beguil'd:
While our sportings are as free
    As the nurse's with the child.

Common beauties stay fifteen;
    Such as yours should swifter move;
Whose fair blossoms are too green
    Yet for lust, but not for love.

Love as much the snowy lamb
    Or the wanton kid does prize,
As the lusty bull or ram,
    For his morning sacrifice.

Now then love me: time may take
    Thee before thy time away:
Of this need we'll virtue make,
    And learn love before we may.

So we win of doubtful fate;
    And, if good she to us meant,
We that good shall antedate,
    Or, if ill, that ill prevent.

Thus as kingdoms, frustrating
    Other titles to their crown,
In the cradle crown their king,
    So all foreign claims to drown;

So, to make all rivals vain,
    Now I crown thee with my love:
Crown me with thy love again,
    And we both shall monarchs prove.

The Picture of Little T. C.
in a Prospect of Flowers

See with what simplicity
This nymph begins her golden days!
In the green grass she loves to lie,
And there with her fair aspect tames
The wilder flow'rs, and gives them names:
But only with the roses plays;
        And them does tell
What color best becomes them, and what smell.

Who can foretell for what high cause
This darling of the gods was born!
Yet this is she whose chaster laws
The wanton love shall one day fear,
And, under her command severe,
See his bow broke and ensigns torn.
           Happy, who can
Appease this virtuous enemy of man!

O then let me in time compound,
And parley with those conquering eyes;
Ere they have tri'd their force to wound,
Ere, with their glancing wheels, they drive
In triumph over hearts that strive,
And them that yield but more despise.
           Let me be laid,
Where I may see thy glories from some shade.

Meantime, whilst every verdant thing
Itself does at thy beauty charm,
Reform the errors of the spring;
Make that the tulips may have share
Of sweetness, seeing they are fair;
And roses of their thorns disarm;
           But most procure
That violets may a longer age endure.

But, O young beauty of the woods,
Whom nature courts with fruits and flow'rs,
Gather the flow'rs, but spare the buds;
Lest Flora, angry at thy crime,
To kill her infants in their prime,
Do quickly make th' example yours;
           And, ere we see,
Nip in the blossom all our hopes and thee.

The Garden

How vainly men themselves amaze
To win the palm, the oak, or bays,
And their incessant labors see
Crown'd from some single herb or tree,
Whose short and narrow verged shade
Does prudently their toils upbraid;

While all flow'rs and all trees do close
To weave the garlands of repose.

Fair Quiet, have I found thee here,
And Innocence, thy sister dear!
Mistaken long, I sought you then
In busy companies of men.

Your sacred plants, if here below,
Only among the plants will grow.
Society is all but rude
To this delicious solitude.

No white nor red was ever seen
So am'rous as this lovely green.
Fond lovers, cruel as their flame,
Cut in these trees their mistress' name.
Little, alas, they know, or heed,
How far these beauties hers exceed!
Fair trees! wheres'e'er your barks I wound,
No name shall but your own be found.

When we have run our passion's heat,
Love hither makes his best retreat.
The gods, that mortal beauty chase,
Still in a tree did end their race.
Apollo hunted Daphne so,
Only that she might laurel grow.
And Pan did after Syrinx speed,
Not as a nymph, but for a reed.

What wond'rous life in this I lead!
Ripe apples drop about my head;
The luscious clusters of the vine
Upon my mouth do crush their wine;
The nectarine and curious peach
Into my hands themselves do reach;
Stumbling on melons, as I pass,
Ensnar'd with flow'rs, I fall on grass.

Meanwhile the mind, from pleasure less,
Withdraws into its happiness:
The mind, that ocean where each kind
Does straight its own resemblance find;
Yet it creates, transcending these,
Far other worlds, and other seas;

Annihilating all that's made
To a green thought in a green shade.

Here at the fountain's sliding foot,
Or at some fruit tree's mossy root,
Casting the body's vest aside,
My soul into the boughs does glide:

There like a bird it sits, and sings,
Then whets and combs its silver wings;
And, till prepar'd for longer flight,
Waves in its plumes the various light.

Such was that happy Garden-state,
While man there walk'd without a mate:
After a place so pure, and sweet,
What other help could yet be meet!
But 'twas beyond a mortal's share
To wander solitary there:
Two paradises 'twere in one
To live in Paradise alone.

How well the skillful gard'ner drew
Of flow'rs and herbs this dial new;
Where from above the milder sun
Does through a fragrant zodiac run;
And, as it works, th' industrious bee
Computes its time as well as we.
How could such sweet and wholesome hours
Be reckon'd but with herbs and flow'rs!

Bermudas

Where the remote Bermudas ride
In th' ocean's bosom unespi'd,
From a small boat, that row'd along,
The list'ning winds receiv'd this song.
    "What should we do but sing his praise
That led us through the wat'ry maze,
Unto an isle so long unknown,
And yet far kinder than our own?
Where he the huge sea-monsters wracks,
That lift the deep upon their backs.
He lands us on a grassy stage;
Safe from the storms and prelates' rage.

He gave us this eternal spring,
Which here enamels everything;
And sends the fowls to us in care,
On daily visits through the air.
He hangs in shades the orange bright,
Like golden lamps in a green night.
And does in the pom'granates close,
Jewels more rich than Ormus shows.
He makes the figs our mouths to meet,
And throws the melons at our feet.
But apples plants of such a price,
No tree could ever bear them twice.
With cedars, chosen by his hand,
From Lebanon, he stores the land.
And makes the hollow seas that roar
Proclaim the ambergris on shore.
He cast (of which we rather boast)
The Gospel's pearl upon our coast,
And in these rocks for us did frame
A temple, where to sound his Name.
Oh, let our voice his praise exalt,
Till it arrive at heaven's vault:
Which thence (perhaps) rebounding, may
Echo beyond the Mexique Bay."
Thus sung they, in the English boat,
An holy and a cheerful note,
And all the way, to guide their chime,
With falling oars they kept the time.

A Dialogue Between the Resolvèd Soul and Created Pleasure

Courage, my Soul, now learn to wield
The weight of thine immortal shield.
Close on thy head thy helmet bright.
Balance thy sword against the fight.
See where an army, strong as fair,
With silken banners spreads the air.
Now, if thou be'st that thing divine,
In this day's combat let it shine:
And show that nature wants an art
To conquer one resolvèd heart.

PLEASURE

Welcome the creation's guest,
Lord of earth, and Heaven's heir.
Lay aside that warlike crest,
And of nature's banquet share:
Where the souls of fruits and flow'rs
Stand prepar'd to heighten yours.

SOUL

I sup above, and cannot stay
To bait so long upon the way.

PLEASURE

On these downy pillows lie,
Whose soft plumes will thither fly:
On these roses stow'd so plain
Lest one leaf thy side should strain.

SOUL

My gentler rest is on a thought,
Conscious of doing what I ought.

PLEASURE

If thou be'st with perfumes pleas'd,
Such as oft the gods appeas'd,
Thou in fragrant clouds shalt show
Like another god below.

SOUL

A Soul that knows not to presume
Is Heaven's and its own perfume.

PLEASURE

Everything does seem to vie
Which should first attract thine eye:
But since none deserves that grace,
In this crystal view *thy* face.

SOUL

When the Creator's skill is priz'd,
The rest is all but earth disguis'd.

PLEASURE

Hark how music then prepares
For thy stay these charming airs,
Which the posting winds recall,
And suspend the river's fall.

SOUL
Had I but any time to lose,
On this I would it all dispose.
Cease, Tempter. None can chain a mind
Whom this sweet chordage cannot bind.

CHORUS
Earth cannot show so brave a sight
As when a single Soul does fence
The batteries of alluring sense,
And Heaven views it with delight.
   Then persevere: for still new charges sound:
   And if thou overcom'st thou shalt be crown'd.

PLEASURE
All this fair, and soft, and sweet,
   Which scatteringly doth shine,
Shall within one beauty meet,
   And she be only thine.

SOUL
If things of sight such heavens be,
What heavens are those we cannot see?

PLEASURE
Wheresoe'er thy foot shall go
   The minted gold shall lie,
Till thou purchase all below,
   And want new worlds to buy.

SOUL
Wer't not a price who'd value gold?
And that's worth nought that can be sold.

PLEASURE
Wilt thou all the glory have
   That war or peace commend?
Half the world shall be thy slave,
   The other half thy friend.

SOUL
What friends, if to my self untrue?
What slaves, unless I captive you?

PLEASURE
Thou shalt know each hidden cause,
   And see the future time:

Try what depth the center draws,
    And then to Heaven climb.

SOUL

None thither mounts by the degree
Of knowledge, but humility.

CHORUS

Triumph, triumph, victorious Soul;
The world has not one pleasure more:
The rest does lie beyond the pole,
And is thine everlasting store.

A Dialogue Between the Soul and Body

SOUL

O who shall from this dungeon raise
A Soul enslav'd so many ways?
With bolts of bones, that fetter'd stands
In feet; and manacled in hands.
Here blinded with an eye; and there
Deaf with the drumming of an ear.
A Soul hung up, as 'twere, in chains
Of nerves, and arteries, and veins.
Tortur'd, besides each other part,
In a vain head, and double heart.

BODY

    O who shall me deliver whole
From bonds of this tyrannic Soul?
Which, stretch'd upright, impales me so,
That mine own precipice I go;
And warms and moves this needless frame:
(A fever could but do the same.)
And, wanting where its spite to try,
Has made me live to let me die.
A body that could never rest,
Since this ill spirit it possess'd.

SOUL

    What magic could me thus confine
Within another's grief to pine?
Where whatsoever it complain,
I feel, that cannot feel, the pain.
And all my care itself employs

That to preserve, which me destroys:
Constrain'd not only to endure
Diseases, but, what's worse, the cure:
And ready oft the port to gain,
Am shipwreck'd into health again.

BODY
   But physic yet could never reach
The maladies thou me dost teach;
Whom first the cramp of hope does tear:
And then the palsy shakes of fear.
The pestilence of love does heat:
Or hatred's hidden ulcer eat.

Joy's cheerful madness does perplex:
Or sorrow's other madness vex.
Which knowledge forces me to know;
And memory will not forgo.
What but a Soul could have the wit
To build me up for sin so fit?
So architects do square and hew
Green trees that in the forest grew.

On a Drop of Dew

See how the orient dew,
Shed from the bosom of the morn
   Into the blowing roses,
Yet careless of its mansion new,
For the clear region where 'twas born
   Round in itself encloses:
   And in its little globe's extent
Frames as it can its native element.
   How it the purple flow'r does slight,
     Scarce touching where it lies,
   But gazing back upon the skies,
     Shines with a mournful light,
      Like its own tear,
Because so long divided from the sphere.
   Restless it rolls and unsecure,
     Trembling lest it grow impure:
   Till the warm sun pity its pain,
And to the skies exhale it back again.
     So the soul, that drop, that ray

Of the clear fountain of eternal day,
Could it within the human flow'r be seen,
 Rememb'ring still its former height,
 Shuns the sweet leaves and blossoms green;
 And, recollecting its own light,
Does, in its pure and circling thoughts, express
The greater heaven in an heaven less.
 In how coy a figure wound,
 Every way it turns away:
 So the world excluding round,
 Yet receiving in the day.
 Dark beneath, but bright above:
 Here disdaining, there in love.
 How loose and easy hence to go:
 How girt and ready to ascend.
 Moving but on a point below,
 It all about does upwards bend.
Such did the manna's sacred dew distill;
White, and entire, though congeal'd and chill.
Congeal'd on earth: but does, dissolving, run
Into the glories of th' Almighty Sun.

Eyes and Tears

 How wisely Nature did decree,
 With the same eyes to weep and see!
 That, having view'd the object vain,
 They might be ready to complain.

 And, since the self-deluding sight
 In a false angle takes each height,
 These tears, which better measure all,
 Like wat'ry lines and plummets fall.

 Two tears, which sorrow long did weigh
 Within the scales of either eye,
 And then paid out in equal poise,
 Are the true price of all my joys.

 What in the world most fair appears,
 Yea, even laughter, turns to tears:
 And all the jewels which we prize,
 Melt in these pendants of the eyes.

I have through every garden been,
Amongst the red, the white, the green;
And yet from all the flow'rs I saw
No honey but these tears could draw.

So the all-seeing sun each day
Distills the world with chemic ray;
But finds the essence only showers,
Which straight in pity back he powers.

Yet happy they whom grief doth bless,
That weep the more, and see the less:
And, to preserve their sight more true,
Bathe still their eyes in their own dew.

So Magdalen, in tears more wise
Dissolv'd those captivating eyes,
Whose liquid chains could flowing meet
To fetter her Redeemer's feet.

Not full sails hasting loaden home,
Nor the chaste lady's pregnant womb,
Nor Cynthia teeming shows so fair
As two eyes swoll'n with weeping are.

The sparkling glance that shoots desire,
Drench'd in these waves, does lose its fire.
Yea, oft the Thund'rer pity takes
And here the hissing lightning slakes.

The incense was to Heaven dear,
Not as a perfume, but a tear.
And stars show lovely in the night,
But as they seem the tears of light.

Ope then, mine eyes, your double sluice,
And practice so your noblest use.
For others too can see, or sleep;
But only human eyes can weep.

Now like two clouds dissolving, drop,
And at each tear in distance stop:
Now like two fountains trickle down:
Now like two floods o'erturn and drown.

Thus let your streams o'erflow your springs,
Till eyes and tears be the same things:
And each the other's difference bears;
These weeping eyes, those seeing tears.

The Coronet

When for the thorns with which I long, too long,
   With many a piercing wound,
   My Savior's head have crown'd,
I seek with garlands to redress that wrong:
   Though every garden, every mead,
I gather flow'rs (my fruits are only flow'rs),

   Dismantling all the fragrant towers
That once adorn'd my shepherdess's head.
And now when I have summ'd up all my store,
   Thinking (so I myself deceive)
   So rich a chaplet thence to weave
As never yet the King of Glory wore:
   Alas, I find the serpent old
   That, twining in his speckled breast,
   About the flow'rs disguis'd does fold,
   With wreaths of fame and interest.
Ah, foolish man, that would'st debase with them,
And mortal glory, Heaven's diadem!
But thou who only couldst the serpent tame,
Either his slipp'ry knots at once untie,
And disentangle all his winding snare,
Or shatter too with him my curious frame:
And let these wither, so that he may die,
Though set with skill and chosen out with care,
That they, while thou on both their spoils dost tread,
May crown thy feet, that could not crown thy head.

An Horatian Ode Upon Cromwell's Return from Ireland

The forward youth that would appear
Must now forsake his muses dear,
   Nor in the shadows sing
   His numbers languishing.
'Tis time to leave the books in dust,
And oil th' unusèd armor's rust,
   Removing from the wall
   The cors'let of the hall.
So restless Cromwell could not cease
In the inglorious arts of peace,
   But through advent'rous war
   Urgèd his active star.

And, like the three-fork'd lightning, first
Breaking the clouds where it was nurst,
   Did thorough his own side
   His fiery way divide.
For 'tis all one to courage high
The emulous or enemy;
   And with such to enclose
   Is more than to oppose.
Then burning through the air he went,
And palaces and temples rent:
   And Cæsar's head at last
   Did through his laurels blast.
'Tis madness to resist or blame
The force of angry Heaven's flame:
   And, if we would speak true,
   Much to the man is due
Who, from his private gardens, where
He liv'd reservèd and austere,
   As if his highest plot
   To plant the bergamot,
Could by industrious valor climb
To ruin the great work of time,
   And cast the kingdom old
   Into another mold.
Though justice against fate complain,
And plead the ancient rights in vain:
   But those do hold or break
   As men are strong or weak.
Nature that hateth emptiness,
Allows of penetration less:
   And therefore must make room
   Where greater spirits come.
What field of all the Civil Wars
Where his were not the deepest scars?
   And Hampton* shows what part
   He had of wiser art.
Where, twining subtle fears with hope,
He wove a net of such a scope,
   That Charles himself might chase

Hampton: this line and the several that follow refer to the flight of Charles I from
Hampton to Carisbrooke in 1647 and his execution in 1650.

To Caresbrook's narrow case.
That thence the Royal Actor born
The tragic scaffold might adorn:
  While round the armèd bands
  Did clap their bloody hands.
He nothing common did or mean
Upon that memorable scene:
  But with his keener eye
  The axe's edge did try:
Nor call'd the gods with vulgar spite
To vindicate his helpless right,
  But bow'd his comely head,
  Down as upon a bed.
This was that memorable hour
Which first assur'd the forcèd pow'r.
  So when they did design
  The Capitol's first line,
A bleeding head where they begun
Did fright the architects to run;
  And yet in that the state
  Foresaw its happy fate.
And now the Irish are asham'd
To see themselves in one year tam'd:
  So much one man can do,
  That does both act and know.
They can affirm his praises best,
And have, though overcome, confess'd
  How good he is, how just,
  And fit for highest trust:
Nor yet grown stiffer with command,
But still in the Republic's hand:
  How fit he is to sway
  That can so well obey.
He to the Commons' feet presents
A kingdom, for his first year's rents:
  And, what he may, forbears
  His fame to make it theirs:
And has his sword and spoils ungirt,
To lay them at the public's skirt.
  So when the falcon high
  Falls heavy from the sky,
She, having kill'd, no more does search,
But on the next green bough to perch;

Where, when he first does lure,
The falc'ner has her sure.
What may not then our Isle presume
While victory his crest does plume!
What may not others fear
If thus he crown each year!
A Cæsar he ere long to Gaul,
To Italy an Hannibal,

And to all states not free
Shall climacteric be.
The Pict no shelter now shall find
Within his particolored mind;
But from this valor sad
Shrink underneath the plaid:
Happy if in the tufted brake
The English hunter him mistake;
Nor lay his hounds in near
The Caledonian deer.
But thou the war's and fortune's son
March indefatigably on;
And for the last effect
Still keep thy sword erect:
Besides the force it has to fright
The spirits of the shady night,
The same arts that did gain
A pow'r must it maintain.

Upon Appleton House

TO MY LORD FAIRFAX[*]
Within this sober frame expect
Work of no foreign architect;
That unto caves the quarries drew,
And forests did to pastures hew;
Who of his great design in pain
Did for a model vault his brain,
Whose columns should so high be rais'd
To arch the brows that on them gaz'd.

---

*Marvell resided for two years at Nun Appleton House, the family seat of Sir Thomas
Fairfax, as tutor to Fairfax's daughter Mary.

Why should of all things man unrul'd
Such unproportion'd dwellings build?
The beasts are by their dens express'd,
And birds contrive an equal nest;
The low-roof'd tortoises do dwell
In cases fit of tortoise-shell:
No creature loves an empty space;
Their bodies measure out their place.

But he, superfluously spread,
Demands more room alive than dead,
And in his hollow palace goes
Where winds as he themselves may lose.
What need of all this marble crust
T' impark the wanton mote of dust,
That thinks by breadth the world t' unite
Though the first builders fail'd in height?

But all things are composèd here
Like Nature, orderly and near:
In which we the dimensions find
Of that more sober age and mind,
When larger-sizèd men did stoop
To enter at a narrow loop;
As practicing, in doors so strait,
To strain themselves through Heavens' gate.

And surely when the after age
Shall hither come in pilgrimage,
These sacred places to adore,
By Vere and Fairfax trod before,
Men will dispute how their extent
Within such dwarfish confines went,
And some will smile at this, as well
As Romulus his bee-like cell.

Humility alone designs
Those short but admirable lines,
By which, ungirt and unconstrain'd,
Things greater are in less contain'd.
Let others vainly strive t' immure
The circle in the quadrature!
These holy mathematics can
In ev'ry figure equal man.

Yet thus the laden house does sweat,
And scarce endures the master great:
But where he comes the swelling hall
Stirs, and the square grows spherical;
More by his magnitude distress'd,
Than he is by its straitness press'd;
And too officiously it slights
That in itself which him delights.

So honor better lowness bears
Than that unwonted greatness wears.
Height with a certain grace does bend,
But low things clownishly ascend.
And yet what needs there here excuse,
Where ev'rything does answer use?
Where neatness nothing can condemn,
Nor pride invent what to contemn?

A stately frontispiece of poor
Adorns without the open door:
Nor less the rooms within commends
Daily new furniture of friends.
The house was built upon the place
Only as for a mark of grace;
And for an inn to entertain
Its lord a while, but not remain.

Him Bishops-Hill, or Denton may,
Or Bilbrough, better hold than they,
But Nature here hath been so free
As if she said "leave this to me."
Art would more neatly have defac'd
What she had laid so sweetly waste;
In fragrant gardens, shady woods,
Deep meadows, and transparent floods.

While with slow eyes we these survey,
And on each pleasant footstep stay,
We opportunely may relate
The progress of this house's fate.
A nunnery first gave it birth;
For virgin buildings oft brought forth.
And all that neighbor-ruin shows
The quarries whence this dwelling rose.

Near to this gloomy cloister's gates
There dwelt the blooming virgin Thwaites,*
Fair beyond measure, and an heir
Which might deformity make fair.
And oft she spent the summer suns
Discoursing with the subtle nuns.
Whence in these words one to her weav'd
(As 'twere by chance) thoughts long conceiv'd.

"Within this holy leisure we
Live innocently as you see.
These walls restrain the world without,
But hedge our liberty about.
These bars enclose that wider den
Of those wild creatures callèd men.
The cloister outward shuts its gates,
And, from us, locks on them the grates.

"Here we, in shining armor white,
Like virgin Amazons do fight.
And our chaste lamps we hourly trim,
Lest the great Bridegroom find them dim.
Our orient breaths perfumèd are
With incense of incessant pray'r.
And holy water of our tears
Most strangely our complexion clears.

"Not tears of grief; but such as those
With which calm pleasure overflows;
Or pity, when we look on you
That live without this happy vow.
How should we grieve that must be seen
Each one a spouse, and each a queen;
And can in Heaven hence behold
Our brighter robes and crowns of gold?

"When we have prayèd all our beads,
Some one the holy legend reads;
While all the rest with needles paint
The face and graces of the saint.

Thwaites: Isabele Thwaites, Thomas Fairfax's great-great-grandmother. This stanza
and those that follow relate the story of her courtship by William Fairfax. She had
been placed in the Cistercian convent at Appleton by her guardian to prevent the
union.

But what the linen can't receive
They in their lives do interweave.
This work the saints best represents;
That serves for altar's ornaments.

"But much it to our work would add
If here your hand, your face we had:
By it we would Our Lady touch;
Yet thus she you resembles much.

Some of your features, as we sew'd,
Through ev'ry shrine should be bestow'd.
And in one beauty we would take
Enough a thousand saints to make.

"And (for I dare not quench the fire
That me does for your good inspire)
'Twere sacrilege a man t' admit
To holy things, for Heaven fit.
I see the angels in a crown
On you the lilies show'ring down:
And round about you glory breaks,
That something more than human speaks.

"All beauty, when at such a height,
Is so already consecrate.
Fairfax, I know; and long ere this
Have mark'd the youth, and what he is.
But can he such a rival seem
For whom you Heav'n should disesteem?
Ah, no! and 'twould more honor prove
He your devoto were than love.

"Here live belovèd and obey'd:
Each one your sister, each your maid.
And, if our rule seem strictly penn'd,
The rule itself to you shall bend.
Our abbess too, now far in age,
Doth your succession near presage.
How soft the yoke on us would lie,
Might such fair hands as yours it tie!

"Your voice, the sweetest of the choir,
Shall draw Heav'n nearer, raise us higher.
And your example, if our head,
Will soon us to perfection lead.

Those virtues to us all so dear
Will straight grow sanctity when here:
And that, once sprung, increase so fast
Till miracles it work at last.

"Nor is our order yet so nice,
Delight to banish as a vice.
Here pleasure piety doth meet;
One perfecting the other sweet.

So through the mortal fruit we boil
The sugar's uncorrupting oil:
And that which perish'd while we pull
Is thus preservèd clear and full.

"For such indeed are all our arts;
Still handling Nature's finest parts.
Flow'rs dress the altars; for the clothes,
The sea-born amber we compose;
Balms for the griev'd we draw, and pastes
We mold, as baits for curious tastes.
What need is here of man? unless
These as sweet sins we should confess.

"Each night among us to your side
Appoint a fresh and virgin bride;
Whom if Our Lord at midnight find,
Yet neither should be left behind.
Where you may lie as chaste in bed
As pearls together billeted.
All night embracing arm in arm,
Like crystal pure with cotton warm.

"But what is this to all the store
Of joys you see, and may make more!
Try but a while, if you be wise:
The trial neither costs, nor ties."
Now, Fairfax, seek her promis'd faith:
Religion that dispensèd hath;
Which she henceforward does begin;
The nun's smooth tongue has suck'd her in.

Oft, though he knew it was in vain,
Yet would he valiantly complain.
"Is this that sanctity so great,
An art by which you fineli'r cheat?

Hypocrite witches, hence avaunt,
Who though in prison yet enchant!
Death only can such thieves make fast,
As rob though in the dungeon cast.

"Were there but, when this house was made,
One stone that a just hand had laid,
It must have fall'n upon her head
Who first thee from thy faith misled.

And yet, how well soever meant,
With them 'twould soon grow fraudulent:
For like themselves they alter all,
And vice infects the very wall.

"But sure those buildings last not long,
Founded by folly, kept by wrong.
I know what fruit their gardens yield,
When they it think by night conceal'd.
Fly from their vices. 'Tis thy state,
Not thee, that they would consecrate.
Fly from their ruin. How I fear
Though guiltless lest thou perish there."

What should he do? He would respect
Religion, but not right neglect:
For first religion taught him right,
And dazzlèd not but clear'd his sight.
Sometimes resolv'd his sword he draws,
But reverenceth then the laws:
For justice still that courage led;
First from a judge, then soldier bred.

Small honor would be in the storm.
The court him grants the lawful form,
Which licens'd either peace or force
To hinder the unjust divorce.
Yet still the nuns his right debarr'd,
Standing upon their holy guard.
Ill-counsel'd women, do you know
Whom you resist, or what you do?

Is not this he whose offspring fierce
Shall fight through all the universe;

And with successive valor try
France, Poland, either Germany;

Till one, as long since prophesi'd,
His horse through conquer'd Britain ride?
Yet, against fate, his spouse they kept,
And the great race would intercept.

Some to the breach against their foes
Their wooden saints in vain oppose.
Another bolder stands at push
With their old holy-water brush.
While the disjointed abbess threads
The jingling chain-shot of her beads.
But their loud'st cannon were their lungs,
And sharpest weapons were their tongues.

But, waving these aside like flies,
Young Fairfax through the wall does rise.
Then th' unfrequented vault appear'd,
And superstitions vainly fear'd.
The relics false were set to view;
Only the jewels there were true.
But truly bright and holy Thwaites
That weeping at the altar waits.

But the glad youth away her bears,
And to the nuns bequeaths her tears:
Who guiltily their prize bemoan,
Like Gypsies that a child hath stol'n.
Thenceforth (as when th' enchantment ends
The castle vanishes or rends)
The wasting cloister with the rest
Was in one instant dispossess'd.

At the demolishing, this seat
To Fairfax fell as by escheat.*
And what both nuns and founders will'd
'Tis likely better thus fulfill'd.
For if the virgin prov'd not theirs,

---

escheat: forfeiture of property to the lord of the manor.

The cloister yet remainèd hers.
Though many a nun there made her vow,
'Twas no religious house till now.

From that bless'd bed the hero came,
Whom France and Poland yet does fame:
Who, when retirèd here to peace,
His warlike studies could not cease;
But laid these gardens out in sport
In the just figure of a fort;
And with five bastions it did fence,
As aiming one for ev'ry sense.

When in the east the morning ray
Hangs out the colors of the day,
The bee through these known alleys hums,
Beating the dian with its drums.
Then flow'rs their drowsy eyelids raise,
Their silken ensigns each displays,
And dries its pan yet dank with dew,
And fills its flask with odors new.

These, as their governor goes by,
In fragrant volleys they let fly;
And to salute their governess
Again as great a charge they press:
None for the virgin nymph; for she
Seems with the flow'rs a flow'r to be.
And think so still! though not compare
With breath so sweet, or cheek so fair.

Well shot, ye firemen! Oh, how sweet
And round your equal fires do meet;
Whose shrill report no ear can tell,
But echoes to the eye and smell.
See how the flow'rs, as at parade,
Under their colors stand display'd:
Each regiment in order grows,
That of the tulip, pink and rose.

But when the vigilant patrol
Of stars walks round about the pole,
Their leaves, that to the stalks are curl'd,
Seem to their staves the ensigns furl'd.
Then in some flow'r's beloved hut

Each bee as sentinel is shut;
And sleeps so too: but, if once stirr'd,
She runs you through, or asks the word.

Oh thou, that dear and happy isle
The garden of the world ere while,
Thou paradise of four seas,
Which Heaven planted us to please,
But, to exclude the world, did guard
With wat'ry if not flaming sword;
What luckless apple did we taste,
To make us mortal, and thee waste?

Unhappy! shall we never more
That sweet militia restore,
When gardens only had their tow'rs,
And all the garrisons were flow'rs,
When roses only arms might bear,
And men did rosy garlands wear?
Tulips, in several colors barr'd,
Were then the Switzers* of our guard.

The gard'ner had the soldier's place,
And his more gentle forts did trace.
The nursery of all things green
Was then the only magazine.
The winter quarters were the stoves,
Where he the tender plants removes.
But war all this doth overgrow:
We ord'nance, plant and powder sow.

And yet there walks one on the sod
Who, had it pleasèd him and God,
Might once have made our gardens spring
Fresh as his own and flourishing.
But he preferr'd to the Cinque Ports†
These five imaginary forts:
And, in those half-dry trenches, spann'd
Pow'r which the ocean might command.

For he did, with his utmost skill,
Ambition weed, but conscience till.

---

*Switzers: Vatican Swiss Guard.
†Cinque Ports: a group of five towns important for English naval defense.

Conscience, that Heaven-nursèd plant,
Which most our earthly gardens want.
A prickling leaf it bears, and such
As that which shrinks at ev'ry touch;
But flow'rs eternal, and divine,
That in the crowns of saints do shine.

The sight does from these bastions ply,
Th' invisible artillery;
And at proud Cawood Castle seems
To point the battery of its beams.
As if it quarrel'd in the seat
Th' ambition of its prelate great.

But o'er the meads below it plays,
Or innocently seems to gaze.

And now to the abyss I pass
Of that unfathomable grass,
Where men like grasshoppers appear,
But grasshoppers are giants there:
They, in their squeaking laugh, contemn
Us as we walk more low than them:
And, from the precipices tall
Of the green spir's, to us do call.

To see men through this meadow dive,
We wonder how they rise alive.
As, under water, none does know
Whether he fall through it or go.
But, as the mariners that sound
And show upon their lead the ground,
They bring up flow'rs so to be seen,
And prove they've at the bottom been.

No scene that turns with engines strange
Does oft'ner than these meadows change.
For when the sun the grass hath vext,
The tawny mowers enter next;
Who seem like Israelites to be,
Walking on foot through a green sea.
To them the grassy deeps divide,
And crowd a lane to either side.

With whistling scythe, and elbow strong,
These massacre the grass along:
While one, unknowing, carves the rail,
Whose yet unfeather'd quills her fail.
The edge all bloody from its breast
He draws, and does his stroke detest;
Fearing the flesh untimely mow'd
To him a fate as black forebode.

But bloody Thestylis, that waits
To bring the mowing camp their cates,
Greedy as kites has truss'd it up,
And forthwith means on it to sup:
When on another quick she lights,
And cries, he call'd us Israelites;
But now, to make his saying true,
Rails rain for quails, for manna dew.

Unhappy birds! what does it boot
To build below the grass's root;
When lowness is unsafe as height,
And chance o'ertakes what scapeth spite?
And now your orphan parents' call
Sounds your untimely funeral.
Death-trumpets creak in such a note,
And 'tis the sourdine* in their throat.

Or sooner hatch or higher build:
The mower now commands the field;
In whose new traverse seemeth wrought
A camp of battle newly fought:
Where, as the meads with hay, the plain
Lies quilted o'er with bodies slain:
The women that with forks it fling,
Do represent the pillaging.

And now the careless victors play,
Dancing the triumphs of the hay;
Where every mower's wholesome heat

*_sourdine_: a low-sounding trumpet.

Smells like an Alexander's sweat.
Their females fragrant as the mead
Which they in fairy circles tread:
When at their dance's end they kiss,
Their new-made hay not sweeter is.

When after this 'tis pil'd in cocks,
Like a calm sea it shows the rocks:
We wond'ring in the river near
How boats among them safely steer.
Or, like the desert Memphis sand,
Short pyramids of hay do stand.
And such the Roman camps do rise
In hills for soldiers' obsequies.

This scene again withdrawing brings
A new and empty face of things;
A level'd space, as smooth and plain,
As clothes for Lely* stretch'd to stain.

The world when first created sure
Was such a table rase and pure.
Or rather such is the toril
Ere the bulls enter at Madril.

For to this naked equal flat,
Which levellers take pattern at,
The villagers in common chase
Their cattle, which it closer rase;
And what below the scythe increast
Is pinch'd yet nearer by the beast.
Such, in the painted world, appear'd
Davenant with th' universal herd.†

They seem within the polish'd grass
A landscape drawn in looking glass,
And shrunk in the huge pasture show
As spots, so shap'd, on faces do.
Such fleas, ere they approach the eye,
In multiplying glasses lie.

Lely: a noted English cloth dyer.
†*Davenant with th' universal herd*: the reference is to a painting of the Six Days of
  Creation.

They feed so wide, so slowly move,
As constellations do above.

Then, to conclude these pleasant acts,
Denton sets ope its cataracts,
And makes the meadow truly be
(What it but seem'd before) a sea.
For, jealous of its Lord's long stay,
It tries t' invite him thus away.
The river in itself is drown'd,
And isles th' astonish'd cattle round.

Let others tell the paradox,
How eels now bellow in the ox;
How horses at their tails do kick,
Turn'd as they hang to leeches quick;
How boats can over bridges sail,
And fishes do the stables scale.
How salmons trespassing are found;
And pikes are taken in the pound.

But I, retiring from the flood,
Take sanctuary in the wood;
And, while it lasts, my self embark
In this yet green, yet growing ark;
Where the first carpenter might best
Fit timber for his keel have press'd,
And where all creatures might have shares,
Although in armies, not in pairs.

The double wood of ancient stocks
Link'd in so thick an union locks,
It like two pedigrees appears,
On one hand Fairfax, th' other Veres:
Of whom though many fell in war,
Yet more to Heaven shooting are:
And, as they Nature's cradle deck'd,
Will in green age her hearse expect.

When first the eye this forest sees
It seems indeed as wood not trees:
As if their neighborhood so old
To one great trunk them all did mold.
There the huge bulk takes place, as meant
To thrust up a fifth element;

And stretches still so closely wedg'd
As if the night within were hedg'd.

Dark all without it knits; within
It opens passable and thin;
And in as loose an order grows,
As the Corinthean porticoes.
The arching boughs unite between
The columns of the temple green;
And underneath the wingèd choirs
Echo about their tunèd fires.

The nightingale does here make choice
To sing the trials of her voice.
Low shrubs she sits in, and adorns
With music high the squatted thorns.
But highest oaks stoop down to hear,
And list'ning elders prick the ear.
The thorn, lest it should hurt her, draws
Within the skin its shrunken claws.

But I have for my music found
A sadder, yet more pleasing sound:
The stock-doves, whose fair necks are grac'd
With nuptial rings, their ensigns chaste;
Yet always, for some cause unknown,
Sad pair unto the elms they moan.
O why should such a couple mourn,
That in so equal flames do burn!

Then as I careless on the bed
Of gelid strawberries do tread,
And through the hazels thick espy
The hatching throstle's shining eye,
The heron from the ash's top
The eldest of its young lets drop,
As if it stork-like did pretend
That tribute to its Lord to send.

But most the hewel's wonders are,
Who here has the holt-felster's care.
He walks still upright from the root,
Meas'ring the timber with his foot;
And all the way, to keep it clean,
Doth from the bark the wood-moths glean
He, with his beak, examines well
Which fit to stand and which to fell.

The good he numbers up, and hacks;
As if he mark'd them with the ax.
But where he, tinkling with his beak,
Does find the hollow oak to speak,
That for his building he designs,
And through the tainted side he mines.
Who could have thought the tallest oak
Should fall by such a feeble stroke!

Nor would it, had the tree not fed
A traitor-worm, within it bred.
(As first our flesh corrupt within
Tempts impotent and bashful sin.)
And yet that worm triumphs not long,
But serves to feed the hewel's young.
While the oak seems to fall content,
Viewing the treason's punishment.

Thus I, easy philosopher,
Among the birds and trees confer:
And little now to make me, wants
Or of the fowls, or of the plants.
Give me but wings as they, and I
Straight floating on the air shall fly:
Or turn me but, and you shall see
I was but an inverted tree.

Already I begin to call
In their most learned original:
And where I language want, my signs
The bird upon the bough divines;
And more attentive there doth sit
Than if she were with lime-twigs knit.
No leaf does tremble in the wind
Which I returning cannot find.

Out of these scatter'd Sibyl's leaves
Strange prophecies my fancy weaves:
And in one history consumes,
Like Mexique paintings, all the plumes.
What Rome, Greece, Palestine, ere said

I in this light mosaic read.
Thrice happy he who, not mistook,
Hath read in Nature's mystic book.
And see how chance's better wit
Could with a mask my studies hit!

The oak-leaves me embroider all,
Between which caterpillars crawl:
And ivy, with familiar trails,
Me licks, and clasps, and curls, and hales.
Under this antic cope I move
Like some great prelate of the grove.

Then, languishing with ease, I toss
On pallets swoll'n of velvet moss;
While the wind, cooling through the boughs,
Flatters with air my panting brows.
Thanks for my rest, ye mossy banks,
And unto you cool Zephyrs, thanks,
Who, as my hair, my thoughts too shed,
And winnow from the chaff my head.

How safe, methinks, and strong, behind
These trees have I encamp'd my mind;
Where beauty, aiming at the heart,
Bends in some tree its useless dart;
And where the world no certain shot
Can make, or me it toucheth not.
But I on it securely play,
And gall its horsemen all the day.

Bind me, ye woodbines, in your twines,
Curl me about, ye gadding vines,
And oh so close your circles lace,
That I may never leave this place:
But, lest your fetters prove too weak,
Ere I your silken bondage break,
Do you, O brambles, chain me too,
And courteous briars, nail me through.

Here in the morning tie my chain,
Where the two woods have made a lane;
While, like a guard on either side,
The trees before their Lord divide;
This, like a long and equal thread,
Betwixt two labyrinths does lead.
But, where the floods did lately drown,
There at the ev'ning stake me down.

For now the waves are fall'n and dri'd,
And now the meadows fresher dy'd;
Whose grass, with moister color dash'd,

Seems as green silks but newly wash'd.
No serpent new nor crocodile
Remains behind our little Nile;
Unless itself you will mistake,
Among these meads the only snake.

See in what wanton harmless folds
It ev'rywhere the meadow holds;
And its yet muddy back doth lick,
Till as a crystal mirror slick,
Where all things gaze themselves, and doubt
If they be in it or without.
And for his shade which therein shines,
Narcissus-like, the sun too pines.

Oh what a pleasure 'tis to hedge
My temples here with heavy sedge;
Abandoning my lazy side,
Stretch'd as a bank unto the tide;
Or to suspend my sliding foot
On the osier's underminèd root,
And in its branches tough to hang,
While at my lines the fishes twang!

But now away my hooks, my quills,
And angles, idle utensils.
The young Maria walks tonight:
Hide, trifling youth, thy pleasures slight.
'Twere shame that such judicious eyes
Should with such toys a man surprise;
She that already is the law
Of all her sex, her age's awe.

See how loose Nature, in respect
To her, itself doth recollect;
And everything so whisht and fine,
Starts forthwith to its bonne mine.
The sun himself, of her aware,
Seems to descend with greater care;
And lest she see him go to bed,
In blushing clouds conceals his head.

So when the shadows laid asleep
From underneath these banks do creep,
And on the river as it flows
With eben shuts begin to close;

The modest halcyon comes in sight,
Flying betwixt the day and night;
And such an horror calm and dumb,
Admiring Nature does benumb.

The viscous air, wheres'ere she fly,
Follows and sucks her azure dye;
The jellying stream compacts below,
If it might fix her shadow so;
The stupid fishes hang, as plain
As flies in crystal overta'en;
And men the silent scene assist,
Charm'd with the sapphire-wingèd mist.

Maria such, and so doth hush
The world, and through the ev'ning rush.
No new-born comet such a train
Draws through the sky, nor star new-slain.
For straight those giddy rockets fail,
Which from the putrid earth exhale,
But by her flames, in Heaven tri'd,
Nature is wholly vitrifi'd.

'Tis she that to these gardens gave
That wondrous beauty which they have;
She straightness on the woods bestows;
To her the Meadow sweetness owes;
Nothing could make the river be
So crystal-pure but only she;
She yet more pure, sweet, straight, and fair,
Than gardens, woods, meads, rivers are.

Therefore what first she on them spent,
They gratefully again present.
The meadow carpets where to tread;
The garden flow'rs to crown her head;
And for a glass the limpid brook,
Where she may all her beauties look;
But, since she would not have them seen,
The wood about her draws a screen.

For she, to higher beauties rais'd,
Disdains to be for lesser prais'd.
She counts her beauty to converse
In all the languages as hers;

Nor yet in those herself employs
But for the wisdom, not the noise;
Nor yet that wisdom would affect,
But as 'tis Heaven's dialect.

Blest nymph! that couldst so soon prevent
Those trains by youth against thee meant;
Tears (wat'ry shot that pierce the mind);
And sighs (love's cannon charg'd with wind);
True praise (that breaks through all defence);
And feign'd complying innocence;
But knowing where this ambush lay,
She scap'd the safe, but roughest way.

This 'tis to have been from the first
In a domestic Heaven nurst,
Under the discipline severe
Of Fairfax, and the starry Vere;
Where not one object can come nigh
But pure, and spotless as the eye;
And goodness doth itself entail
On females, if there want a male.

Go now, fond sex, that on your face
Do all your useless study place,
Nor once at vice your brows dare knit
Lest the smooth forehead wrinkled sit:
Yet your own face shall at you grin,
Thorough the black-bag of your skin;
When knowledge only could have fill'd
And virtue all those furrows till'd.

Hence she with graces more divine
Supplies beyond her sex the line;
And, like a sprig of mistletoe,
On the Fairfacian oak does grow;
Whence, for some universal good,
The priest shall cut the sacred bud;
While her glad parents most rejoice,
And make their destiny their choice.

Meantime, ye fields, springs, bushes, flow'rs,
Where yet she leads her studious hours
(Till fate her worthily translates,

And find a Fairfax for our Thwaites),
Employ the means you have by her,
And in your kind yourselves prefer;
That, as all virgins she precedes,
So you all woods, streams, gardens, meads.

For you Thessalian Tempe's seat
Shall now be scorn'd as obsolete;
Aranjuez, as less, disdain'd;
The Bel-Retiro as constrain'd;*
But name not the Idalian Grove,
For 'twas the seat of wanton love;
Much less the dead's Elysian Fields,
Yet nor to them your beauty yields.

'Tis not, what once it was, the world,
But a rude heap together hurl'd;
All negligently overthrown,
Gulfs, deserts, precipices, stone,
Your lesser world contains the same.
But in more decent order tame;
You Heaven's center, nature's lap,
And paradise's only map.

But now the salmon-fishers moist
Their leathern boats begin to hoist;
And, like Antipodes in shoes,
Have shod their heads in their canoes.
How tortoise-like, but not so slow,
These rational amphibii go?
Let 's in: for the dark hemisphere
Does now like one of them appear.

GEORGE HERBERT (1593–1633)

Exclusively a religious poet, George Herbert was educated at Westminster School and Trinity College, Cambridge. Talented as an orator and poet, Herbert might have achieved great things in the law or government service. He rejected a secular career, however, and instead took Holy Orders in 1630. He spent the three remaining years of his life as rector of the parish of Bemerton near Salisbury. In *The Temple*

---

*Thessalian Tempe, Aranjuez, Bel-Retiro: famous gardens.

(1633), his best-known collection of poems, Herbert experimented with nearly every form of verse in plumbing the psychology of his religious experiences. Meticulously constructed, his poems reveal an extraordinary versatility and incisive intelligence coping with the agonies and joys of a tormented soul struggling toward peace with God. As the critic H. J. C. Grierson has noted, ". . . Herbert is a sincere and sensitive poet, and an accomplished artist elaborating his argumentative strain or little allegories and conceits with felicitous completeness [and] a finished and delicate harmony."

Jordan (1)

Who says that fictions only and false hair
Become a verse? Is there in truth no beauty?
Is all good structure in a winding stair?
May no lines pass except they do their duty
    Not to a true, but painted chair?

Is it no verse except enchanted groves
And sudden arbors shadow coarse-spun lines?
Must purling streams refresh a lover's loves?
Must all be veiled, while he that reads, divines,
    Catching the sense at two removes?

Shepherds are honest people; let them sing;
Riddle who list for me, and pull for prime;
I envy no man's nightingale or spring,
Nor let them punish me with loss of rhyme,
    Who plainly say, My God, my King.

Jordan (2)

When first my lines of heav'nly joys made mention,
Such was their luster, they did so excel,

That I sought out quaint words and trim invention;
My thoughts began to burnish, sprout, and swell,
Curling with metaphors a plain intention,
Decking the sense as if it were to sell.

Thousands of notions in my brain did run,
Off'ring their service, if I were not sped.
I often blotted what I had begun,
This was not quick enough, and that was dead.
Nothing could seem too rich to clothe the sun,
Much less those joys which trample on his head.

As flames do work and wind when they ascend,
So did I weave myself into the sense.
But while I bustled, I might hear a friend
Whisper, How wide is all this long pretense!
There is in love a sweetness ready penned,
Copy out only that, and save expense.

The British Church

I joy, dear mother, when I view
Thy perfect lineaments, and hue
    Both sweet and bright.
Beauty in thee takes up her place,
And dates her letters from thy face,
    When she doth write.

A fine aspect in fit array,
Neither too mean nor yet too gay,
    Shows who is best.
Outlandish looks may not compare,
For all they either painted are,
    Or else undressed.

She on the hills which wantonly
Allureth all, in hope to be
    By her preferred,
Hath kissed so long her painted shrines,
That ev'n her face by kissing shines,
    For her reward.

She in the valley is so shy
Of dressing, that her hair doth lie
    About her ears;
While she avoids her neighbor's pride,
She wholly goes on th' other side,
    And nothing wears.

She is simple

But, dearest mother, what those miss,
The mean, thy praise and glory is
    And long may be.
Blessed be God, whose love it was
To double-moat thee with his grace,
    And none but thee.

The Son

Let foreign nations of their language boast,
What fine variety each tongue affords;
I like our language, as our men and coast;
Who cannot dress it well, want wit, not words.

a simple language

How neatly do we give one only name
To parents' issue and the sun's bright star.
A son is light and fruit, a fruitful flame
Chasing the father's dimness, carried far
From the first man in th' East to fresh and new
Western discov'ries of posterity.
So in one word our Lord's humility
We turn upon him in a sense most true;
   For what Christ once in humbleness began,
   We him in glory call, The Son of Man.

new world

The Altar

A broken altar, Lord, thy servant rears,
Made of a heart and cémented with tears;
   Whose parts are as thy hand did frame;
   No workman's tool hath touched the same.
                A   heart   alone
                Is   such   a   stone
                As   nothing   but
                Thy power doth cut.
                Wherefore each part
                Of my hard heart
                Meets in this frame
                To praise thy name;
   That if I chance to hold my peace,
   These stones to praise thee may not cease.
Oh, let thy blessed sacrifice be mine,
And sanctify this altar to be thine.

The Church Floor

Mark you the floor? That square and speckled stone,
                Which looks so firm and strong,
                      Is Patience;

Virtus

And th' other black and grave, wherewith each one
        Is checkered all along,
            Humility.

The gentle rising, which on either hand
        Leads to the choir above,
            Is Confidence.

But the sweet cement, which in one sure band
        Ties the whole frame, is Love
            And Charity.

        Hither sometimes sin steals, and stains
        The marble's neat and curious veins;
But all is cleansëd when the marble weeps.
        Sometimes death, puffing at the door,
        Blows all the dust about the floor;
But while he thinks to spoil the room, he sweeps.
        Blest be the architect whose art
        Could build so strong in a weak heart.

Easter Wings

Lord, who createdst man in wealth and store,
        Though foolishly he lost the same,
            Decaying more and more
                Till he became
                    Most poor;
                    With thee
                Oh, let me rise
            As larks harmoniously,
        And sing this day thy victories;
Then shall the fall further the flight in me.

        My tender age in sorrow did begin;
        And still with sicknesses and shame
            Thou didst so punish sin,
                That I became
                    Most thin.
                    With thee
                Let me combine,
        And feel this day thy victory;
        For if I imp my wing on thine,
Affliction shall advance the flight in me.

Lent

Welcome, dear feast of Lent! Who loves not thee,
He loves not temperance or authority,
   But is composed of passion.
The Scriptures bid us fast; the Church says, Now;
Give to thy mother what thou wouldst allow
   To ev'ry corporation.

The humble soul, composed of love and fear,
Begins at home and lays the burden there,
   When doctrines disagree.
He says, in things which use hath justly got,
I am a scandal to the church, and not
   The Church is so to me.

True Christians should be glad of an occasion
To use their temperance, seeking no evasion
   When good is seasonable;
Unless authority, which should increase
The obligation in us, make it less,
   And power itself disable.

Besides the cleanness of sweet abstinence,
Quick thoughts and motions at a small expense,
   A face not fearing light;
Whereas in fullness there are sluttish fumes,
Sour exhalations, and dishonest rheums,
   Revenging the delight.

Then those same pendant profits, which the spring
And Easter intimate, enlarge the thing
   And goodness of the deed.
Neither ought other men's abuse of Lent
Spoil the good use, lest by that argument
   We forfeit all our creed.

It's true we cannot reach Christ's forti'th day,
Yet to go part of that religious way
   Is better than to rest.
We cannot reach our Savior's purity,
Yet are we bid, Be holy ev'n as he.
   In both let's do our best.

Who goeth in the way which Christ hath gone,
Is much more sure to meet with him than one

    That traveleth byways.
Perhaps my God, though he be far before,
May turn and take me by the hand, and more
    May strengthen my decays.

Yet, Lord, instruct us to improve our fast
By starving sin, and taking such repast
    As may our faults control;
That ev'ry man may revel at his door,
Not in his parlor; banqueting the poor,
    And among those his soul.

Sunday

    O day most calm, most bright,
The fruit of this, the next world's bud,
Th' indorsement of supreme delight,
Writ by a friend, and with his blood,
The couch of time, care's balm and bay;

The week were dark but for thy light,
    Thy torch doth show the way.

    The other days and thou
Make up one man, whose face thou art,
Knocking at heaven with thy brow.
The worky-days are the back part,
The burden of the week lies there,
Making the whole to stoop and bow
    Till thy release appear.

    Man had straight forward gone
To endless death, but thou dost pull
And turn us round to look on one
Whom, if we were not very dull,
We could not choose but look on still,
Since there is no place so alone
    The which he doth not fill.

    Sundays the pillars are
On which heav'n's palace archèd lies;
The other days fill up the spare
And hollow room with vanities.

They are the fruitful beds and borders
In God's rich garden; that is bare
　　Which parts their ranks and orders.

　　The Sundays of man's life,
Threaded together on time's string,
Make bracelets to adorn the wife
Of the eternal glorious king.
On Sunday heaven's gate stands ope,
Blessings are plentiful and rife,
　　More plentiful than hope.

　　This day my Savior rose,
And did enclose this light for his;
That, as each beast his manger knows,
Man might not of his fodder miss.
Christ hath took in this piece of ground,
And made a garden there for those
　Who want herbs for their wound.

　　The rest of our creation
Our great Redeemer did remove
With the same shake which at his passion

Did th' earth and all things with it move.
As Samson bore the doors away,
Christ's hands, though nailed, wrought our salvation,
　　And did unhinge that day.

　　The brightness of that day
We sullied by our foul offence;
Wherefore that robe we cast away,
Having a new at his expense,
Whose drops of blood paid the full price
That was required to make us gay,
　　And fit for paradise.

　　Thou art a day of mirth;
And where the week-days trail on ground,
Thy flight is higher, as thy birth.
O let me take thee at the bound,
Leaping with thee from sev'n to sev'n,
Till that we both, being tossed from earth,
　　Fly hand in hand to heav'n.

Church Music

Sweetest of sweets, I thank you! when displeasure
   Did through my body wound my mind,
You took me thence, and in your house of pleasure
   A dainty lodging me assigned.

Now I in you without a body move,
   Rising and falling with your wings.
We both together sweetly live and love,
   Yet say sometimes, God help poor kings.

Comfort, I'll die; for if you post from me,
   Sure I shall do so and much more.
But if I travel in your company,
   You know the way to heaven's door.

To All Angels and Saints

O glorious spirits, who after all your bands
See the smooth face of God without a frown
   Or strict commands,
Where ev'ryone is king, and hath his crown,
If not upon his head, yet in his hands.

Not out of envy or maliciousness
Do I forbear to crave your special aid;
   I would address
My vows to thee most gladly, blessed Maid,
And Mother of my God, in my distress;

Thou art the holy mine whence came the gold,
The great restorative for all decay
   In young and old;
Thou art the cabinet where the jewel lay;
Chiefly to thee would I my soul unfold.

But now, alas, I dare not, for our King,
Whom we do all jointly adore and praise,
   Bids no such thing;
And where his pleasure no injunction lays,
'Tis your own case, ye never move a wing.

All worship is prerogative, and a flower
Of his rich crown from whom lies no appeal
   At the last hour.
Therefore we dare not from his garland steal
To make a posy for inferior power.

Although, then, others court you, if ye know
What's done on earth, we shall not fare the worse
    Who do not so;
Since we are ever ready to disburse,
If anyone our Master's hand can show.

Man

    My God, I heard this day
That none doth build a stately habitation
    But he that means to dwell therein.
    What house more stately hath there been,
Or can be, than is man, to whose creation
      All things are in decay?

      For man is ev'rything,
And more: he is a tree, yet bears no fruit;
    A beast, yet is, or should be, more;
    Reason and speech we only bring;
Parrots may thank us if they are not mute,
      They go upon the score.

    Man is all symmetry,
Full of proportions, one limb to another,
    And all to all the world besides.
    Each part may call the farthest brother,
For head with foot hath private amity,
      And both with moons and tides.

    Nothing hath got so far,
But man hath caught and kept it as his prey:
    His eyes dismount the highest star;
    He is in little all the sphere;
Herbs gladly cure our flesh, because that they
      Find their acquaintance there.

    For us the winds do blow,
The earth doth rest, heav'n move, and fountains flow.
    Nothing we see but means our good,
    As our delight, or as our treasure;
The whole is either our cupboard of food,
      Or cabinet of pleasure.

    The stars have us to bed;
Night draws the curtain, which the sun withdraws;
    Music and light attend our head;

All things unto our flesh are kind
In their descent and being, to our mind
    In their ascent and cause.

    Each thing is full of duty:
Waters united are our navigation;
    Distinguishëd, our habitation;
    Below, our drink; above, our meat;
Both are our cleanliness. Hath one such beauty?
    Then how are all things neat!

    More servants wait on man
Than he'll take notice of: in ev'ry path
    He treads down that which doth befriend him
    When sickness makes him pale and wan.
Oh, mighty love! Man is one world and hath
    Another to attend him.

    Since then, my God, thou hast
So brave a palace built, O dwell in it,
    That it may dwell with thee at last!
    Till then afford us so much wit
That as the world serves us we may serve thee,
    And both thy servants be.

Affliction

When first thou didst entice to thee my heart,
    I thought the service brave;
So many joys I writ down for my part,
    Besides what I might have
Out of my stock of natural delights,
Augmented with thy gracious benefits.

I looked on thy furniture so fine,
    And made it fine to me;
Thy glorious household-stuff did me entwine,
    And 'tice me unto thee.
Such stars I counted mine: both heav'n and earth
Paid me my wages in a world of mirth.

What pleasures could I want whose king I served,
    Where joys my fellows were?
Thus argued into hopes, my thoughts reserved
    No place for grief or fear.
Therefore my sudden soul caught at the place,
And made her youth and fierceness seek thy face.

At first thou gav'st me milk and sweetness;
   I had my wish and way;
My days were strawed with flowers and happiness,
   There was no month but May.
But with my years, sorrow did twist and grow,
And made a party unawares for woe.

My flesh began unto my soul in pain:
   Sicknesses cleave my bones;
Consuming agues dwell in ev'ry vein,
   And tune my breath to groans.
Sorrow was all my soul; I scarce believed,
Till grief did tell me roundly, that I lived.

When I got health thou took'st away my life,
   And more, for my friends die.
My mirth and edge was lost; a blunted knife
   Was of more use than I.
Thus thin and lean, without a fence or friend,
I was blown through with ev'ry storm and wind.

Whereas my birth and spirit rather took
   The way that takes the town,
Thou didst betray me to a ling'ring book
   And wrap me in a gown.
I was entangled in the world of strife
Before I had the power to change my life.

Yet, for I threatened oft the siege to raise,
   Not simp'ring all mine age,
Thou often didst with academic praise
   Melt and dissolve my rage.
I took thy sweetened pill till I came near;
I could not go away, nor persevere.

Yet lest perchance I should too happy be
   In my unhappiness,
Turning my purge to food, thou throwest me
   Into more sicknesses.
Thus doth thy power cross-bias me, not making
Thine own gift good, yet me from my ways taking.

Now I am here, what thou wilt do with me
   None of my books will show.
I read and sigh and wish I were a tree,
   For sure then I should grow
To fruit or shade. At least some bird would trust
Her household to me, and I should be just.

Yet, though thou troublest me, I must be meek;
    In weakness must be stout.
Well, I will change the service and go seek
    Some other master out.
Ah, my dear God! though I am clean forgot,
Let me not love thee if I love thee not.

Frailty

Lord, in my silence how do I despise
    What upon trust
Is styled honor, riches, or fair eyes,
    But is fair dust!
  I surname them gilded clay,
  Dear earth, fine grass or hay.
In all I think my foot doth ever tread
    Upon their head.

But when I view abroad both regiments,
    The world's and thine,
Thine clad with simpleness and sad events,
    The other fine,
  Full of glory and gay weeds,
  Brave language, braver deeds;
That which was dust before doth quickly rise,
    And prick mine eyes.

O brook not this, lest if what even now
    My foot did tread,
Affront those joys wherewith thou didst endow
    And long since wed
  My poor soul, ev'n sick of love;
  It may a Babel prove,
Commodious to conquer heav'n and thee,
    Planted in me.

Nature

  Full of rebellion, I would die,
  Or fight, or travel, or deny
  That thou hast aught to do with me.
    O tame my heart!
    It is thy highest art
  To captivate strongholds to thee.

If thou shalt let this venom lurk
And in suggestions fume and work,
My soul will turn to bubbles straight,
    And thence by kind
    Vanish into a wind,
Making thy workmanship deceit.

O smooth my rugged heart, and there
Engrave thy rev'rend law and fear.
Or make a new one, since the old
    Is sapless grown,
    And a much fitter stone
To hide my dust than thee to hold.

The Pearl

MATTHEW XIII

I know the ways of learning, both the head
And pipes that feed the press, and make it run;
What reason hath from nature borrowëd,
Or of itself, like a good housewife, spun
In laws and policy; what the stars conspire;
What willing nature speaks, what forced by fire;
Both th'old discoveries and the new-found seas,
The stock and surplus, cause and history;
All these stand open, or I have the keys—
            Yet I love thee.

I know the ways of honor: what maintains
The quick returns of courtesy and wit;
In vies of favors whether party gains
When glory swells the heart and moldeth it
To all expressions both of hand and eye,
Which on the world a true-love-knot may tie,
And bear the bundle wheresoe'er it goes;
How many drams of spirit there must be
To sell my life unto my friends or foes—
            Yet I love thee.

I know the ways of pleasure: the sweet strains,
The lullings and the relishes of it;
The propositions of hot blood and brains;
What mirth and music mean; what love and wit
Have done these twenty hundred years and more;

I know the projects of unbridled store;
My stuff is flesh, not brass; my senses live,
And grumble oft that they have more in me
Than he that curbs them, being but one to five—
  Yet I love thee.

I know all these and have them in my hand;
Therefore not seelèd but with open eyes
I fly to thee, and fully understand
Both the main sale and the commodities;
And at what rate and price I have thy love,

With all the circumstances that may move.
Yet through the labyrinths, not my groveling wit,
But thy silk twist let down from heav'n to me
Did both conduct and teach me how by it
  To climb to thee.

The Pulley

  When God at first made man,
Having a glass of blessings standing by,
Let us, said he, pour on him all we can.
Let the world's riches, which dispersèd lie,
  Contract into a span.

  So strength first made a way,
Then beauty flowed, then wisdom, honor, pleasure.
When almost all was out, God made a stay,
Perceiving that alone of all his treasure
  Rest in the bottom lay.

  For if I should, said he,
Bestow this jewel also on my creature,
He would adore my gifts instead of me,
And rest in nature, not the God of nature;
  So both should losers be.

  Yet let him keep the rest,
But keep them with repining restlessness.
Let him be rich and weary, that at least,
If goodness lead him not, yet weariness
  May toss him to my breast.

Peace

Sweet Peace, where dost thou dwell? I humbly crave
      Let me once know.
  I sought thee in a secret cave,
    And asked if Peace were there,
A hollow wind did seem to answer, No,
      Go seek elsewhere.

I did, and going did a rainbow note.
      Surely, thought I,
  This is the lace of Peace's coat,
    I will search out the matter;
But while I looked, the clouds immediately
      Did break and scatter.

Then went I to a garden and did spy
      A gallant flower,
  The crown imperial. Sure, said I,
    Peace at the root must dwell.
But when I digged, I saw a worm devour
      What showed so well.

At length I met a rev'rend good old man,
      Whom when for Peace
  I did demand, he thus began:
    There was a prince of old
At Salem dwelt, who lived with good increase
      Of flock and fold.

He sweetly lived, yet sweetness did not save
      His life from foes.
  But after death out of his grave
    There sprang twelve stalks of wheat;
Which many wond'ring at, got some of those
      To plant and set.

It prospered strangely and did soon disperse
      Through all the earth;
  For they that taste it do rehearse
    That virtue lies therein,
A secret virtue bringing peace and mirth
      By flight of sin.

Take of this grain, which in my garden grows,
　　　　And grows for you;
　　Make bread of it, and that repose
　　And peace which ev'rywhere
With so much earnestness you do pursue,
　　　　Is only there.

Conscience

　　Peace, prattler, do not lour!
Not a fair look but thou dost call it foul.
Not a sweet dish but thou dost call it sour.
　　　　Music to thee doth howl.
　　By list'ning to thy chatting fears,
　　I have both lost mine eyes and ears.

　　　　Prattler, no more, I say!
My thoughts must work, but like a noiseless sphere;
Harmonious peace must rock them all the day,
　　　　No room for prattlers there.
　　If thou persistest, I will tell thee
　　That I have physic to expel thee.

　　　　And the receipt shall be
My Savior's blood. Whenever at his board
I do but taste it, straight it cleanseth me
　　　　And leaves thee not a word;
　　No, not a tooth or nail to scratch,
　　And at my actions carp or catch.

　　　　Yet if thou talkest still,
Besides my physic know there's some for thee;
Some wood and nails to make a staff or bill
　　　　For those that trouble me.
　　The bloody cross of my dear Lord
　　Is both my physic and my sword.

Discipline

　　　Throw away thy rod,
　　　Throw away thy wrath.
　　　　　O my God,
　　　Take the gentle path.

For my heart's desire
Unto thine is bent;
   I aspire
To a full consent.

   Not a word or look
I affect to own,
     But by book,
And thy book alone.

   Though I fail, I weep.
Though I halt in pace,
     Yet I creep
To the throne of grace.

   Then let wrath remove;
Love will do the deed,
     For with love
Stony hearts will bleed.

   Love is swift of foot.
Love's a man of war,
     And can shoot,
And can hit from far.

   Who can 'scape his bow?
That which wrought on thee,
     Brought thee low,
Needs must work on me.

   Throw away thy rod.
Though man frailties hath,
     Thou art God.
Throw away thy wrath.

Redemption

Having been tenant long to a rich Lord,
   Not thriving, I resolved to be bold,
   And make a suit unto him to afford
A new small-rented lease and cancel the old.
In heaven at his manor I him sought.
    They told me there that he was lately gone
    About some land which he had dearly bought

Long since on earth, to take possession.
I straight returned, and knowing his great birth,
Sought him accordingly in great resorts,
In cities, theaters, gardens, parks, and courts.
At length I heard a ragged noise and mirth
Of thieves and murderers; there I him espied,
Who straight, Your suit is granted, said, and died.

Love

Love bade me welcome, yet my soul drew back,
  Guilty of dust and sin.
But quick-eyed Love, observing me grow slack
  From my first entrance in,
Drew nearer to me, sweetly questioning
  If I lacked anything.

A guest, I answered, worthy to be here.
  Love said, You shall be he.
I, the unkind, the ungrateful? ah, my dear,
  I cannot look on thee.
Love took my hand and smiling did reply,
  Who made the eyes but I?

Truth, Lord, but I have marred them; let my shame
  Go where it doth deserve.
And know you not, says Love, who bore the blame?
  My dear, then I will serve.
You must sit down, says Love, and taste my meat.
  So I did sit and eat.

The Priesthood

Blest order, which in power doth so excel,
  That with th' one hand thou liftest to the sky,
And with the other throwest down to hell
  In thy just censures; fain would I draw nigh,
Fain put thee on, exchanging my lay-sword
    For that of th' holy word.

But thou art fire, sacred and hallowed fire,
  And I but earth and clay. Should I presume
To wear thy habit, the severe attire,
  My slender compositions might consume.
I am both foul and brittle, much unfit
    To deal in holy writ.

Yet have I often seen, by cunning hand
And force of fire, what curious things are made
Of wretched earth. Where once I scorned to stand,
That earth is fitted by the fire and trade
Of skillful artists for the boards of those
  Who make the bravest shows.

But since those great ones, be they ne'er so great,
Come from the earth from whence those vessels come,
So that at once both feeder, dish, and meat
Have one beginning and one final sum;
I do not greatly wonder at the sight,
  If earth in earth delight.

But th' holy men of God such vessels are
As serve him up who all the world commands.
When God vouchsafeth to become our fare,
Their hands convey him who conveys their hands.
Oh, what pure things, most pure, must those things be
  Who bring my God to me!

Wherefore I dare not, put forth my hand
To hold the Ark, although it seem to shake
Through th' old sins and new doctrines of our land.
Only since God doth often vessels make
Of lowly matter for high uses meet,
  I throw me at his feet.

There will I lie until my maker seek
For some mean stuff whereon to show his skill.
Then is my time. The distance of the meek
Doth flatter power. Lest good come short of ill
In praising might, the poor do by submission
  What pride by opposition.

Aaron

Holiness on the head,
  Light and perfections on the breast,
Harmonious bells below, raising the dead
  To lead them unto life and rest:
    Thus are true Aarons dressed.

Profaneness in my head,
  Defects and darkness in my breast,
A noise of passions ringing me for dead

Unto a place where is no rest:
    Poor priest, thus am I dressed.

Only another head
I have, another heart and breast,
Another music, making live not dead,
    Without whom I could have no rest:
      In him I am well dressed.

Christ is my only head,
My alone only heart and breast,
My only music, striking me ev'n dead,
    That to the old man I may rest,
      And be in him new dressed.

So holy in my head,
Perfect and light in my dear breast,
My doctrine tuned by Christ, who is not dead,
    But lives in me while I do rest,
      Come people! Aaron's dressed.

The Windows

Lord, how can man preach thy eternal word?
    He is a brittle crazy glass,
Yet in thy temple thou dost him afford
    This glorious and transcendent place
    To be a window, through thy grace.

But when thou dost anneal in glass thy story,
    Making thy life to shine within
The holy preacher's, then the light and glory
    More rev'rend grows, and doth more win;
    Which else shows wat'rish, bleak, and thin.

Doctrine and life, colors and light in one,
    When they combine and mingle, bring
A strong regard and awe; but speech alone
    Doth vanish like a flaring thing,
    And in the ear, not conscience, ring.

The Call

Come, my way, my truth, my life;
    Such a way as gives us breath,
Such a truth as ends all strife,
    Such a life as killeth death.

Come, my light, my feast, my strength;
    Such a light as shows a feast,
Such a feast as mends in length,
    Such a strength as makes his guest.

Come, my joy, my love, my heart;
    Such a joy as none can move,
Such a love as none can part,
    Such a heart as joys in love.

The Odor

2 CORINTHIANS II

How sweetly doth My Master sound! My Master!
    As ambergris leaves a rich scent
      Unto the taster,
    So do these words a sweet content,
An oriental fragrancy, My Master.

With these all day I do perfume my mind,
    My mind ev'n thrust into them both,
      That I might find
    What cordials make this curious broth,
This broth of smells, that feeds and fats my mind.

My Master, shall I speak? Oh, that to thee
    My servant! were a little so,
      As flesh may be,
    That these two words might creep and grow
To some degree of spiciness to thee!

Then should the pomander, which was before
    A speaking sweet, mend by reflection
      And tell me more;
    For pardon of my imperfection
Would warm and work it sweeter than before.

For when My Master, which alone is sweet
    And ev'n in my unworthiness pleasing,
      Shall call and meet
    My servant, as thee not displeasing,
That call is but the breathing of the sweet.

This breathing would with gains by sweet'ning me,
    As sweet things traffic when they meet,
      Return to thee;
    And so this new commerce and sweet
Should all my life employ and busy me.

A True Hymn

My joy, my life, my crown!
My heart was meaning all the day
　　Somewhat it fain would say;
And still it runneth mutt'ring up and down
With only this, My joy, my life, my crown.

　　Yet slight not these few words.
If truly said they take part
　　Among the best in art.
The fineness which a hymn or psalm affords
Is when the soul unto the lines accords.

　　He who craves all the mind,
And all the soul, and strength, and time,
　　If the words only rhyme,
Justly complains that somewhat is behind
To make his verse, or write a hymn in kind.

　　Whereas if th' heart be moved,
Although the verse be somewhat scant,
　　God doth supply the want,
As when th' heart says, sighing to be approved,
Oh, could I love! and stops, God writeth, Loved.

Dullness

Why do I languish thus, drooping and dull,
　　As if I were all earth?
O give me quickness, that I may with mirth
　　Praise thee brim-full!

The wanton lover in a curious strain
　　Can praise his fairest fair,
And with quaint metaphors her curlèd hair
　　Curl o'er again.

Thou art my loveliness, my life, my light,
　　Beauty alone to me.
Thy bloody death and undeserved makes thee
　　Pure red and white.

When all perfections as but one appear—
　　That, those, thy form doth show—
The very dust where thou dost tread and go
　　Makes beauties here.

Where are my lines then, my approaches, views?
    Where are my window-songs?
Lovers are still pretending, and ev'n wrongs
    Sharpen their muse.

But I am lost in flesh, whose sugared lies
    Still mock me and grow bold.
Sure thou didst put a mind there, if I could
    Find where it lies.

Lord, clear thy gift, that with a constant wit
    I may but look towards thee.
Look only, for to love thee, who can be,
    What angel, fit?

The Collar

I struck the board and cried, No more!
        I will abroad.
What? Shall I ever sigh and pine?
My lines and life are free: free as the road,
    Loose as the wind, as large as store.
        Shall I be still in suit?
Have I no harvest but a thorn
To let me blood, and not restore
What I have lost with cordial fruit?
            Sure there was wine
    Before my sighs did dry it; there was corn
        Before my tears did drown it.
    Is the year only lost to me?
        Have I no bays to crown it?
No flowers, no garlands gay? All blasted?
        All wasted?
    Not so, my heart! But there is fruit,
        And thou hast hands.
    Recover all thy sigh-blown age
On double pleasures. Leave thy cold dispute
Of what is fit and not. Forsake thy cage,
        Thy rope of sands,
Which petty thoughts have made, and made to thee
    Good cable, to enforce and draw,
            And be thy law,
While thou didst wink and wouldst not see.

Away! Take heed!
I will abroad.
Call in thy death's head there. Tie up thy fears.
He that forbears
To suit and serve his need
Deserves his load.
But as I raved and grew more fierce and wild
At every word,
Me thoughts I heard one calling, Child!
And I replied, My Lord.

The Flower

How fresh, O Lord, how sweet and clean
Are thy returns! Ev'n as the flowers in spring,
To which, besides their own demean,
The late-past frosts tributes of pleasure bring.
Grief melts away
Like snow in May,
As if there were no such cold thing.

Who would have thought my shriveled heart
Could have recovered greenness? It was gone
Quite underground, as flowers depart
To see their mother-root when they have blown;
Where they together
All the hard weather,
Dead to the world, keep house unknown.

These are thy wonders, Lord of power,
Killing and quick'ning, bringing down to hell
And up to heaven in an hour;
Making a chiming of a passing bell.

We say amiss
This or that is;
Thy word is all, if we could spell.

Oh, that I once past changing were,
Fast in thy paradise, where no flower can wither!
Many a spring I shoot up fair,
Off'ring at heav'n, growing and groaning thither;
Nor doth my flower
Want a spring shower,
My sins and I joining together.

But while I grow in a straight line,
Still upwards bent, as if heav'n were mine own,
   Thy anger comes, and I decline.
What frost to that? What pole is not the zone
       Where all things burn,
       When thou dost turn,
And the least frown of thine is shown?

And now in age I bud again,
After so many deaths I live and write;
   I once more smell the dew and rain,
And relish versing. O my only light,
       It cannot be
       That I am he
On whom thy tempests fell all night.

These are thy wonders, Lord of love,
To make us see we are but flowers that glide;
   Which when we once can find and prove,
Thou hast a garden for us where to bide.
       Who would be more,
       Swelling through store,
Forfeit their paradise by their pride.

Virtue

Sweet day, so cool, so calm, so bright,
The bridal of the earth and sky;
The dew shall weep thy fall to-night,
     For thou must die.

Sweet rose, whose hue angry and brave
Bids the rash gazer wipe his eye;
Thy root is ever in its grave,
     And thou must die.

Sweet spring, full of sweet days and roses,
A box where sweets compacted lie;
My music shows ye have your closes,
     And all must die.

Only a sweet and virtuous soul,
Like seasoned timber, never gives;
But though the whole world turn to coal,
     Then chiefly lives.

RICHARD CRASHAW (1613–1649)

The son of a Puritan preacher, Crashaw took his B.A. at Cambridge, and later became a Catholic (ca. 1645). Official hostility towards Catholics, however, forced Crashaw to flee England for France and then Italy, where he obtained a post in a Cardinal's household. He was later appointed sub-canon of the Cathedral of Santa Casa in Loretto. His finest verse, on religious themes, is characterized by a near-Baroque extravagance, embodying radiant spirit, ardor, music and "happy fireworks," especially embodied in his famous "Hymn to Sainte Teresa." As Grierson notes, "His conceits are more after the confectionery manner of the Italians than the scholastic or homely manner of the followers of Donne." Yet in Crashaw's poetry is found the "joy of the toubled soul who has found rest and a full expansion of heart in the rediscovery of a faith and ritual and order which give entire satisfaction to the imagination and affections."

On Mr. G. Herbert's Book, Entitled The Temple of Sacred Poems, Sent to a Gentlewoman

Know you, fair, on what you look:
Divinest love lies in this book,
Expecting fire from your eyes
To kindle this his sacrifice.
When your hands untie these strings,
Think you've an angel by the wings,
One that gladly will be nigh
To wait upon each morning sigh,
To flutter in the balmy air
Of your well-perfumëd prayer.
These white plumes of his he'll lend you,
Which every day to heaven will send you
To take acquaintance of the sphere
And all the smooth-faced kindred there.
   And though Herbert's name do owe
   These devotions, fairest, know
   That while I lay them on the shrine
   Of your white hand, they are mine.

A Hymn to the Name and Honor of the Admirable
Saint Teresa

Foundress of the reformation of the Discalced Carmelites, both men and women. A woman for angelical height of speculation, for masculine courage of performance, more than a woman, who yet a child outran maturity, and durst plot a martyrdom.

> Love, thou art absolute sole lord
> Of life and death. To prove the word,
> We'll now appeal to none of all
> Those thy old soldiers, great and tall,
> Ripe men of martyrdom, that could reach down
> With strong arms their triumphant crown,
> Such as could with lusty breath
> Speak loud into the face of death
> Their great Lord's glorious name; to none
> Of those whose spacious bosoms spread a throne
> For love at large to fill; spare blood and sweat,
> And see him take a private seat,
> Making his mansion in the mild
> And milky soul of a soft child.
>   Scarce has she learned to lisp the name
> Of martyr, yet she thinks it shame
> Life should so long play with that breath
> Which spent can buy so brave a death.
> She never undertook to know
> What death with love should have to do;
> Nor has she e'er yet understood
> Why to show love she should shed blood;
> Yet though she cannot tell you why,
> She can love and she can die.
>   Scarce has she blood enough to make
> A guilty sword blush for her sake;
> Yet has she a heart dares hope to prove
> How much less strong is death than love.
>   Be love but there, let poor six years
> Be posed with the maturest fears
> Man trembles at, you straight shall find
> Love knows no nonage, nor the mind.

'Tis love, not years or limbs that can
Make the martyr or the man.
    Love touched her heart, and lo it beats
High, and burns with such brave heats,
Such thirsts to die, as dares drink up
A thousand cold deaths in one cup.
Good reason, for she breathes all fire;
Her weak breast heaves with strong desire
Of what she may with fruitless wishes
Seek for amongst her mother's kisses.
    Since 'tis not to be had at home,
She'll travel to a martyrdom.
No home for hers confesses she
But where she may a martyr be.
    She'll to the Moors, and trade with them
For this unvalued diadem.
She'll offer them her dearest breath,
With Christ's name in 't, in change for death.
She'll bargain with them, and will give
Them God, teach them how to live
In him; or if they this deny,
For him she'll teach them how to die.
So shall she leave amongst them sown
Her Lord's blood, or at least her own.
    Farewell then, all the world, adieu!
Teresa is no more for you.
Farewell, all pleasures, sports, and joys,
Never till now esteemëd toys,
Farewell, whatever dear may be,
Mother's arms or father's knee;
Farewell house and farewell home,
She's for the Moors and martyrdom!
    Sweet, not so fast! lo, thy fair spouse
Whom thou seek'st with so swift vows
Calls thee back, and bids thee come
T' embrace a milder martyrdom.
    Blest powers forbid thy tender life
Should bleed upon a barbarous knife;
Or some base hand have power to race
Thy breast's chaste cabinet and uncase
A soul kept there so sweet; oh no,
Wise heav'n will never have it so:
Thou art love's victim, and must die

A death more mystical and high;
Into love's arms thou shalt let fall
A still surviving funeral.
His is the dart must make the death
Whose stroke shall taste thy hallowed breath;
A dart thrice dipped in that rich flame
Which writes thy spouse's radiant name
Upon the roof of heav'n, where aye
It shines, and with a sovereign ray
Beats bright upon the burning faces
Of souls, which in that name's sweet graces
Find everlasting smiles. So rare,
So spiritual, pure, and fair
Must be th' immortal instrument
Upon whose choice point shall be sent
A life so loved; and that there be
Fit executioners for thee,
The fair'st and first-born sons of fire,
Blest seraphim, shall leave their choir
And turn love's soldiers, upon thee
To exercise their archery.
    Oh, how oft shalt thou complain
Of a sweet and subtle pain,
Of intolerable joys,
Of a death in which who dies
Loves his death, and dies again,
And would forever so be slain,
And lives and dies, and knows not why
To live, but that he thus may never leave to die.
    How kindly will thy gentle heart
Kiss the sweetly killing dart!
And close in his embraces keep
Those delicious wounds, that weep
Balsam to heal themselves with. Thus
When these thy deaths, so numerous,
Shall all at last die into one,
And melt thy soul's sweet mansïon
Like a soft lump of incense, hasted
By too hot a fire, and wasted
Into perfuming clouds, so fast
Shalt thou exhale to heav'n at last
In a resolving sigh; and then,
Oh, what? Ask not the tongues of men;

Angels cannot tell; suffice,
Thyself shall feel thine own full joys
And hold them fast forever. There
So soon as thou shalt first appear,
The moon of maiden stars, thy white
Mistress, attended by such bright
Souls as thy shining self, shall come
And in her first ranks make thee room;
Where 'mongst her snowy family
Immortal welcomes wait for thee.
    Oh, what delight when revealed life shall stand
And teach thy lips heav'n with his hand,
On which thou now mayst to thy wishes
Heap up thy consecrated kisses.
What joys shall seize thy soul when she,
Bending her blessed eyes on thee,
Those second smiles of heaven, shall dart
Her mild rays through thy melting heart!
    Angels, thy old friends, there shall greet thee,
Glad at their own home now to meet thee.
    All thy good works which went before
And waited for thee at the door
Shall own thee there, and all in one
Weave a constellation
Of crowns, with which the King, thy spouse,
Shall build up thy triumphant brows.
    All thy old woes shall now smile on thee,
And thy pains sit bright upon thee;
All thy sorrows here shall shine,
All thy sufferings be divine;
Tears shall take comfort and turn gems,
And wrongs repent to diadems.
Even thy deaths shall live, and new
Dress the soul that erst they slew;
Thy wounds shall blush to such bright scars
As keep account of the Lamb's wars.
    Those rare works where thou shalt leave writ
Love's noble history, with wit
Taught thee by none but him, while here
They feed our souls, shall clothe thine there.
Each heav'nly word by whose hid flame
Our hard hearts shall strike fire, the same
Shall flourish on thy brows, and be

Both fire to us and flame to thee,
Whose light shall live bright in thy face
By glory, in our hearts by grace.
  Thou shalt look round about and see
Thousands of crowned souls throng to be
Themselves thy crown; sons of thy vows,
The virgin-births with which thy sovereign spouse
Made fruitful thy fair soul, go now
And with them all about thee, bow
To him. Put on, he'll say, put on,
My rosy love, that thy rich zone
Sparkling with the sacred flames
Of thousand souls whose happy names
Heav'n keeps upon thy score. Thy bright
Life brought them first to kiss the light
That kindled them to stars. And so
Thou with the Lamb, thy Lord, shalt go,
And whereso'er he sets his white
Steps, walk with him those ways of light
Which who in death would live to see
Must learn in life to die like thee.

Saint Mary Magdalene, or the Weeper

     Hail, sister springs!
   Parents of silver-footed rills!
   Ever-bubbling things!
    Thawing crystal! snowy hills,
Still spending, never spent! I mean
Thy fair eyes, sweet Magdalene!

     Heavens thy fair eyes be;
   Heavens of ever-falling stars;
   'Tis seed-time still with thee,
    And stars thou sow'st, whose harvest dares
Promise the earth to countershine
Whatever makes heav'n's forehead fine.

     But we're deceived all.
   Stars indeed they are, too true,
   For they but seem to fall,
    As heav'n's other spangles do.
It is not for our earth and us
To shine in things so precïous.

Upwards thou dost weep;
Heav'n's bosom drinks the gentle stream;
Where th' milky rivers creep,
Thine floats above, and is the cream.
Waters above th' heav'ns, what they be
We're best taught by thy tears and thee.

Every morn from hence
A brisk cherub something sips,
Whose sacred influence
Adds sweetness to his sweetest lips;
Then to his music, and his song
Tastes of this breakfast all day long.

Not in the evening's eyes,
When they red with weeping are
For the sun that dies,
Sits sorrow with a face so fair;
Nowhere but here did ever meet
Sweetness so sad, sadness so sweet.

When sorrow would be seen
In her brightest majesty,
For she is a queen,
Then is she dressed by none but thee;
Then, and only then, she wears
Her proudest pearls: I mean—thy tears.

The dew no more will weep
The primrose's pale cheek to deck,
The dew no more will sleep,
Nuzzled in the lily's neck;
Much rather would it be thy tear,
And leave them both to tremble here.

There's no need at all
That the balsam-sweating bough
So coyly should let fall
His med'cinable tears, for now
Nature hath learnt t' extract a dew
More sovereign and sweet from you.

Yet let the poor drops weep,
Weeping is the ease of woe,

Softly let them creep,
   Sad that they are vanquished so;
They, though to others no relief,
Balsam may be for their own grief.

   Such the maiden gem
   By the purpling vine put on,
   Peeps from her parent stem
   And blushes at the bridegroom sun.
This wat'ry blossom of thy eyne,
Ripe, will make the richer wine.

   When some new bright guest
   Takes up among the stars a room,
   And heav'n will make a feast,
   Angels with crystal vials come
And draw from these full eyes of thine
Their master's water, their own wine.

   Golden though he be,
   Golden Tagus murmurs though;
   Were his way by thee,
   Content and quiet he would go;
So much more rich would he esteem
Thy silver, than his golden stream.

   Well does the May that lies
   Smiling in thy cheeks, confess
   The April in thine eyes;
   Mutual sweetness they express:
No April e'er lent kinder showers,
Nor May returned more faithful flowers.

   O cheeks! beds of chaste loves
   By your own showers seasonably dashed;
   Eyes! nests of milky doves
   In your own wells decently washed;
O wit of love! that thus could place
Fountain and garden in one face.

   O sweet contest, of woes
   With loves, of tears with smiles disputing!
   O fair and friendly foes,
   Each other kissing and confuting!
While rain and sunshine, cheeks and eyes,
Close in kind contrarieties.

But can these fair floods be
Friends with the bosom fires that fill thee?
Can so great flames agree
Eternal tears should thus distil thee?
O floods, O fires, O suns, O showers!
Mixed and made friends by love's sweet powers.

'Twas his well-pointed dart
That digged these wells and dressed this vine;
And taught the wounded heart
The way into these weeping eyne.
Vain loves, avaunt! bold hands, forbear!
The lamb hath dipped his white foot here.

And now where e'er he strays
Among the Galilean mountains,
Or more unwelcome ways,
He's followed by two faithful fountains,
Two walking baths, two weeping motions,
Portable and compendious oceans.

O thou, thy Lord's fair store!
In thy so rich and rare expenses,
Even when he showed most poor,
He might provoke the wealth of princes;
What prince's wanton'st pride e'er could
Wash with silver, wipe with gold?

Who is that king, but he
Who call'st his crown to be called thine,
That thus can boast to be
Waited on by a wand'ring mine,
A voluntary mint, that strows
Warm silver showers where e'er he goes?

O precious prodigal!
Fair spendthrift of thyself! thy measure,
Merciless love, is all,
Even to the last pearl in thy treasure;
All places, times, and objects be
Thy tears' sweet opportunity.

Does the day-star rise?
Still thy stars do fall and fall.
Does day close his eyes?
Still the fountain weeps for all.

Let night or day do what they will,
Thou hast thy task, thou weepest still.

        Does thy song lull the air?
  Thy falling tears keep faithful time.
  Does thy sweet-breathed prayer
  Up in clouds of incense climb?
Still at each sigh, that is, each stop,
A bead, that is, a tear, does drop.

        At these thy weeping gates,
  Watching their wat'ry motïon,
  Each wingëd moment waits,
  Take his tear and gets him gone;
By thine eye's tinct ennobled thus,
Time lays him up, he's precïous.

        Not, So long she lived,
  Shall thy tomb report of thee;
  But, So long she grieved,
  Thus must we date thy memory:
Others by moments, months, and years,
Measure their ages, thou by tears.

        So do perfumes expire;
  So sigh tormented sweets, oppressed
  With proud unpitying fire;
  Such tears the suff'ring rose that's vexed
With ungentle flames does shed,
Sweating in a too warm bed.

        Say, ye bright brothers,
  The fugitive sons of those fair eyes,
  Your fruitful mothers,
  What make you here? What hopes can 'tice
You to be born? What cause can borrow
You from those nests of noble sorrow?

        Whither away so fast?
  For sure the sordid earth
  Your sweetness cannot taste,
  Nor does the dust deserve your birth.
Sweet, whither haste you then? O say
Why you trip so fast away!

We go not to seek
The darlings of Aurora's bed,
The rose's modest cheek,
Nor the violet's humble head;
Though the field's eyes, too, weepers be
Because they want such tears as we.

Much less mean we to trace
The fortune of inferior gems,
Preferred to some proud face,
Or perched upon feared diadems:
Crowned heads are toys. We go to meet
A worthy object, our Lord's feet.

On the Baptized Ethiopian

Let it no longer be a forlorn hope
To wash an Ethiope.
He's washed: his gloomy skin a peaceful shade
For his white soul is made.
And now, I doubt not, the eternal Dove
A black-faced house will love.

Give to Cæsar . . . and to
God . . . MARK XII

All we have is God's and yet
Cæsar challenges a debt;
Nor hath God a thinner share,
Whatever Cæsar's payments are;
All is God's, and yet 'tis true
All we have is Cæsar's too;
All is Cæsar's, and what odds
So long as Cæsar's self is God's?

But Men Loved Darkness Rather
Than Light JOHN III

The world's light shines; shine as it will,
The world will love its darkness still;
I doubt though when the world's in hell,
It will not love its darkness half so well.

To Pontius Washing His Hands

Thy hands are washed, but oh, the water's spilt
    That labored to have washed thy guilt;
The flood, if any can, that can suffice
    Must have its fountain in thine eyes.

Samson to His Delilah

Could not once blinding me, cruel, suffice?
When first I looked on thee, I lost mine eyes.

To our Lord, upon the Water
Made Wine

Thou water turn'st to wine, fair friend of life;
    Thy foe to cross the sweet arts of thy reign
Distils from thence the tears of wrath and strife,
    And so turns wine to water back again.

Upon the Infant Martyrs

To see both blended in one flood,
The mother's milk, the children's blood,
Makes me doubt if heaven will gather
Roses hence, or lilies rather.

On the Miracle of Loaves

Now Lord, or never, they'll believe on thee,
Thou to their teeth hast proved thy deity.

Upon Lazarus His Tears

Rich Lazarus! richer in those gems, thy tears,
    Than Dives in the robes he wears;
He scorns them now, but oh, they'll suit full well
    With th' purple he must wear in hell.

From Carmen Deo Nostro, 1652

*To the noblest and best of ladies,
the Countess of Denbigh*

*Persuading her to resolution in religion, and to render herself without
further delay into the communion of the Catholic Church*

What heav'n-entreated heart is this,
Stands trembling at the gate of bliss?
Holds fast the door, yet dares not venture
Fairly to open it, and enter;
Whose definition is a doubt
'Twixt life and death, 'twixt in and out.
Say, ling'ring fair, why comes the birth
Of your brave soul so slowly forth?
Plead your pretenses, O you strong
In weakness, why you choose so long
In labor of yourself to lie,
Not daring quite to live nor die.
Ah linger not, loved soul! A slow
And late consent was a long no;
Who grants at last, long time tried
And did his best to have denied.
What magic bolts, what mystic bars
Maintain the will in these strange wars!
What fatal, yet fantastic, bands
Keep the free heart from its own hands!
So when the year takes cold, we see
Poor waters their own prisoners be;
Fettered and locked up fast they lie
In a sad self-captivity.
Th' astonished nymphs their flood's strange fate deplore,
To see themselves their own severer shore.
Thou that alone canst thaw this cold,
And fetch the heart from its stronghold,
Almighty love! end this long war,
And of a meteor make a star.
Oh, fix this fair indefinite,
And 'mongst thy shafts of sovereign light
Choose out that sure decisive dart
Which has the key of this close heart,
Knows all the corners of 't, and can control
The self-shut cabinet of an unsearched soul.

Oh, let it be at last love's hour;
Raise this tall trophy of thy power;
Come once the conquering way, not to confute
But kill this rebel word, irresolute,
That so, in spite of all this peevish strength
Of weakness, she may write, Resolved at length.
Unfold at length, unfold, fair flower,
And use the season of love's shower;
Meet his well-meaning wounds, wise heart!
And haste to drink the wholesome dart,
That healing shaft, which heav'n till now
Hath in love's quiver hid for you.
O dart of love! arrow of light!
O happy you, if it hit right;
It must not fall in vain, it must
Not mark the dry regardless dust.
Fair one, it is your fate, and brings
Eternal worlds upon its wings.
Meet it with wide-spread arms, and see
Its seat your soul's just center be.
Disband dull fears, give faith the day;
To save your life, kill your delay,
It is love's siege, and sure to be
Your triumph, though his victory.
'Tis cowardice that keeps this field,
And want of courage not to yield.
Yield then, O yield, that love may win
The fort at last and let life in;
Yield quickly, lest perhaps you prove
Death's prey, before the prize of love.
This fort of your fair self, if 't be not won,
He is repulsed indeed, but you're undone.

A Song

Lord, when the sense of thy sweet grace
Sends up my soul to seek thy face,
Thy blessed eyes breed such desire
I die in love's delicious fire.
    O love, I am thy sacrifice.

Be still triumphant, blessed eyes;
Still shine on me, fair suns! that I
Still may behold, though still I die.

Though still I die, I live again,
Still longing so to be still slain;

So gainful is such loss of breath,
I die even in desire of death.
   Still live in me this loving strife
Of living death and dying life;
For while though sweetly slayest me,
Dead to myself, I live in thee.

Wishes to His Supposed Mistress

Who e'er she be,
That not impossible she
That shall command my heart and me;

Where e'er she lie,
Locked up from mortal eye
In shady leaves of destiny,

Till that ripe birth
Of studied fate stand forth
And teach her fair steps to our earth,

Till that divine
Idea take a shrine
Of crystal flesh, through which to shine;

Meet you her, my wishes,
Bespeak her to my blisses,
And be ye called my absent kisses.

I wish her beauty
That owes not all his duty
To gaudy tire, nor glist'ring shoe-ty;

Something more than
Taffeta or tissue can,
Or rampant feather, or rich fan;

More than the spoil
Of shop, or silkworm's toil,
Or a bought blush, or a set smile.

A face that's best
By its own beauty dressed,
And can alone command the rest;

A face made up
Out of no other shop
Than what nature's white hand sets ope;

A cheek where youth,
And blood, with pen of truth
Write what the reader sweetly ru'th;

A cheek where grows
More than a morning rose,
Which to no box his being owes;

Lips where all day
A lover's kiss may play,
Yet carry nothing thence away;

Looks that oppress
Their richest tires, but dress
And clothe their simplest nakedness;

Eyes that displaces
The neighbor diamond, and out faces
That sunshine by their own sweet graces;

Tresses that wear
Jewels but to declare
How much themselves more precious are,

Whose native ray
Can tame the wanton day
Of gems, that in their bright shades play—

Each ruby there,
Or pearl that dare appear,
Be its own blush, be its own tear;

A well-tamed heart,
For whose more noble smart
Love may be long choosing a dart;

Eyes that bestow
Full quivers on Love's bow,
Yet pay less arrows than they owe;

Smiles that can warm
The blood, yet teach a charm,
That chastity shall take no harm;

Blushes that been
The burnish of no sin,
Nor flames of aught too hot within;

Joys that confess
Virtue their mistress,
And have no other head to dress;

Fears, fond and flight
As the coy bride's when night
First does the longing lover right;

Tears, quickly fled,
And vain, as those are shed
For a dying maidenhead;

Days that need borrow
No part of their good morrow
From a forespent night of sorrow;

Days that in spite
Of darkness, by the light
Of a clear mind are day all night;

Nights sweet as they,
Made short by lovers' play,
Yet long by th' absence of the day;

Life that dares send
A challenge to his end,
And when it comes say, Welcome friend;

Sidneian showers
Of sweet discourse, whose powers
Can crown old winter's head with flowers;

Soft silken hours,
Open suns, shady bowers,
'Bove all, nothing that lours:

Whate'er delight
Can make day's forehead bright,
Or give down to the wings of night.

In her whole frame
Have nature all the name,
Art and ornament the shame.

Her flattery,
Picture and poesy,
Her counsel her own virtue be.

I wish her store
Of worth may leave her poor
Of wishes, and I wish—no more.

Now if time knows
That her whose radiant brows
Weave them a garland of my vows,

Her whose just bays
My future hopes can raise,
A trophy to her present praise;

Her that dares be
What these lines wish to see:
I seek no further, it is she.

'Tis she, and here,
Lo, I unclothe and clear
My wishes' cloudy character.

May she enjoy it
Whose merit dare apply it
But modesty dares still deny it.

Such worth as this is
Shall fix my flying wishes,
And determine them to kisses.

Let her full glory,
My fancies, fly before ye;
Be ye my fictions, but her story.

Music's Duel

Now westward Sol had spent the richest beams
Of noon's high glory, when hard by the streams
Of Tiber, on the scene of a green plat,
Under protection of an oak, there sat
A sweet lute's master, in whose gentle airs

He lost the day's heat, and his own hot cares.
   Close in the covert of the leaves there stood
A nightingale, come from the neighboring wood,
The sweet inhabitant of each glad tree,
Their muse, their siren, harmless siren she;
There stood she list'ning and did entertain
The music's soft report, and mold the same
In her own murmurs, that whatever mood
His curious fingers lent, her voice made good.
The man perceived his rival and her art;
Disposed to give the light-foot lady sport,
Awakes his lute, and 'gainst the fight to come
Informs it, in a sweet *præludium*
Of closer strains, and ere the war begin
He lightly skirmishes on every string,
Charged with a flying touch; and straightway she
Carves out her dainty voice as readily
Into a thousand sweet distinguished tones,
And reckons up in soft divisïons
Quick volumes of wild notes, to let him know
By that shrill taste, she could do something too.
   His nimble hands' instinct then taught each string
A cap'ring cheerfulness, and made them sing
To their own dance: now negligently rash,
He throws his arm, and with a long-drawn dash
Blends all together; then distinctly trips
From this to that; then quick returning skips
And snatches this again, and pauses there.
She measures every measure, everywhere
Meets art with art; sometimes as if in doubt
Not perfect yet, and fearing to be out,
Trails her plain ditty in one long-spun note,
Through the sleek passage of her open throat,
A clear unwrinkled song; then doth she point it
With tender accents, and severely joint it
By short diminutives, that being reared
In controverting warbles evenly shared,
With her sweet self she wrangles. He, amazed
That from so small a channel should be raised
The torrent of a voice whose melody
Could melt into such sweet variety,
Strains higher yet, that tickled with rare art,
The tattling strings, each breathing in his part,

Most kindly do fall out: the grumbling bass
In surly groans disdains the treble's grace;
The high-perched treble chirps at this, and chides,
Until his finger, moderator, hides
And closes the sweet quarrel, rousing all—
Hoarse, shrill, at once—as when the trumpets call
Hot Mars to th' harvest of death's field, and woo
Men's hearts into their hands. This lesson too
She gives him back; her supple breast thrills out
Sharp airs, and staggers in a warbling doubt
Of dallying sweetness, hovers o'er her skill,
And folds in waved notes with a trembling bill
The pliant series of her slippery song.
Then starts she suddenly into a throng
Of short thick sobs, whose thund'ring volleys float
And roll themselves over her lubric throat
In panting murmurs, stilled out of her breast,
That ever-bubbling spring, the sugared nest
Of her delicious soul, that there does lie
Bathing in streams of liquid melody;
Music's best seed-plot, whence in ripened airs
A golden-headed harvest fairly rears
His honey-dropping tops, plowed by her breath
Which there reciprocally laboreth
In that sweet soil. It seems a holy choir
Founded to the name of great Apollo's lyre,
Whose silver roof rings with the sprightly notes
Of sweet-lipped angel-imps that swill their throats
In cream of morning Helicon, and then
Prefer soft anthems to the ears of men,
To woo them from their beds, still murmuring
That men can sleep while they their matins sing—
Most divine service, whose so early lay
Prevents the eyelids of the blushing day.
There you might hear her kindle her soft voice
In the close murmur of a sparkling noise,
And lay the groundwork of her hopeful song,
Still keeping in the forward stream, so long
Till a sweet whirlwind, striving to get out,
Heaves her soft bosom, wanders round about,
And makes a pretty earthquake in her breast,
Till the fledged notes at length forsake their nest,
Fluttering in wanton shoals, and to the sky,

Winged with their own wild echo's prattling, fly.
She opes the floodgate and lets loose a tide
Of streaming sweetness, which in state doth ride
On the waved back of every swelling strain,
Rising and falling in a pompous train.
And while she thus discharges a shrill peal
Of flashing airs, she qualifies their zeal
With the cool epode of a graver note,
Thus high, thus low, as if her silver throat
Would reach the brazen voice of war's hoarse bird.
Her little soul is ravished, and so poured
Into loose ecstasies that she is placed
Above herself, music's enthusiast.

    Shame now and anger mixed a double stain
In the musician's face. Yet once again,
Mistress, I come; now reach a strain, my lute,
Above her mock, or be forever mute;
Or tune a song of victory to me,
Or to thyself sing thine own obsequy.
So said, his hands sprightly as fire he flings
And with a quavering coyness tastes the strings.
The sweet-lipped sisters, musically frighted,
Singing their fears are fearfully delighted,
Trembling as when Apollo's golden hairs
Are fanned and frizzled in the wanton airs
Of his own breath, which married to his lyre
Doth tune the spheres, and make heaven's self look higher.
From this to that, from that to this, he flies,
Feels music's pulse in all her arteries,
Caught in a net which there Apollo spreads,
His fingers struggle with the vocal threads;
Following those little rills, he sinks into
A sea of Helicon; his hand does go
Those parts of sweetness which with nectar drop,
Softer than that which pants in Hebe's cup.
The humorous strings expound his learnèd touch
By various glosses; now they seem to grutch
And murmur in a buzzing din, then jingle
In shrill-tongued accents, striving to be single.
Every smooth turn, every delicious stroke
Gives life to some new grace; thus doth h' invoke
Sweetness by all her names; thus, bravely thus,
Fraught with a fury so harmonious,

The lute's light genius now doth proudly rise,
Heaved on the surges of swollen rhapsodies,
Whose flourish, meteor-like, doth curl the air
With flash of high-born fancies, here and there
Dancing in lofty measures; and anon
Creeps on the soft touch of a tender tone
Whose trembling murmurs melting in wild airs
Runs to and fro, complaining his sweet cares,
Because those precious mysteries that dwell
In music's ravished soul he dares not tell,
But whisper to the world; thus do they vary
Each string his note, as if they meant to carry
Their master's blest soul, snatched out at his ears
By a strong ecstasy, through all the spheres
Of music's heaven, and seat it there on high
In th' empyræum of pure harmony.
At length, after so long, so loud a strife
Of all the strings, still breathing the best life
Of blest variety attending on
His fingers' fairest revolution
In many a sweet rise, many as sweet a fall,
A full-mouth diapason swallows all.
　　This done, he lists what she would say to this,
And she, although her breath's late exercise
Had dealt too roughly with her tender throat,
Yet summons all her sweet powers for a note.
Alas, in vain! for while, sweet soul, she tries
To measure all those wild diversities
Of chatt'ring strings, by the small size of one
Poor simple voice, raised in a natural tone,
She fails, and failing grieves, and grieving dies.
She dies, and leaves her life the victor's prize,
Falling upon his lute; O fit to have,
That lived so sweetly, dead, so sweet a grave!

HENRY VAUGHAN (1621–1695)

Born in Wales, Henry Vaughan attended Oxford, studied law in
London for two years and later practiced medicine. Although he wrote
some secular poetry, Vaughan's reputation rests on his inspired reli-
gious verse. Reminiscent of Herbert's *The Temple*, Vaughan's religious
poetry is contained in two volumes entitled *Silex Scintillans*, meaning

"The Fiery Flint," a reference to Divine steel striking fire from the poet's heart. Unlike Herbert, his religious and poetic inspiration came not primarily from the church, but from his intimate intuition of the divinity inherent in the natural world. Although not as polished a poet as Herbert, Vaughan nevertheless projects profundity and mystical power, sustained by his vision of eternity as a "great ring of pure and endless light."

Idle Verse

Go, go, quaint follies, sugared sin,
    Shadow no more my door;
I will no longer cobwebs spin,
    I'm too much on the score.

For since amidst my youth and night
    My great preserver smiles,
We'll make a match, my only light,
    And join against their wiles;

Blind, desp'rate fits, that study how
    To dress and trim our shame,
That gild rank poison, and allow
    Vice in a fairer name;

The purls of youthful blood and bowels,
    Lust in the robes of love,
The idle talk of fev'rish souls,
    Sick with a scarf or glove;

Let it suffice my warmer days
    Simpered and shined on you,
Twist not my cypress with your bays,
    Or roses with my yew;

Go, go, seek out some greener thing,
    It snows and freezeth here;
Let nightingales attend the spring,
    Winter is all my year.

Mount of Olives (1)

Sweet sacred hill! on whose fair brow
My Savior sat, shall I allow
    Language to love
And idolize some shade or grove,

Neglecting thee? Such ill-placed wit,
Conceit, or call it what you please,
    Is the brain's fit,
    And mere disease.

Cotswold and Cooper's, both have met
With learned swains, and echo yet
    Their pipes and wit;
But thou sleep'st in a deep neglect,
Untouched by any; and what need
The sheep bleat thee a silly lay,
    That heard'st both reed
    And sheep-ward play?

Yet if poets mind thee well,
They shall find thou art their hill,
    And fountain too,
Their Lord with thee had most to do;
He wept once, walked whole nights on thee,
And from thence, his suff'rings ended,
    Unto glory
    Was attended.

Being there, this spacious ball
Is but his narrow footstool all,

    And what we think
Unsearchable, now with one wink
He doth comprise; but in this air
When he did stay to bear our ill
    And sin, this hill
    Was then his chair.

Mount of Olives (2)

When first I saw true beauty, and thy joys
Active as light, and calm without all noise,
Shined on my soul, I felt through all my powers
Such a rich air of sweets as evening showers,
Fanned by a gentle gale, convey and breathe
On some parched bank, crowned with a flow'ry wreath;
Odors and myrrh and balm in one rich flood
O'erran my heart and spirited my blood;
My thoughts did swim in comforts, and mine eye
Confessed, The world did only paint and lie.

And where before I did no safe course steer,
But wandered under tempests all the year,
Went bleak and bare in body as in mind,
And was blown through by ev'ry storm and wind;
I am so warmed now by this glance on me
That 'midst all storms I feel a ray of thee;
So have I known some beauteous paisage rise
In sudden flowers and arbors to my eyes,
And in the depth and dead of winter bring
To my cold thoughts a lively sense of spring.
    Thus fed by thee, who dost all beings nourish,
My withered leaves again look green, and flourish;
I shine and shelter underneath thy wing,
Where sick with love I strive thy name to sing,
Thy glorious name! which grant I may so do
That these may be thy praise, and my joy too.

The Garland

Thou who dost flow and flourish here below,
To whom a falling star and nine days' glory,
Or some frail beauty, makes the bravest show,
Hark, and make use of this ensuing story.

  When first my youthful, sinful age
    Grew master of my ways,
  Appointing error for my page,
    And darkness for my days,
  I flung away, and with full cry
    Of wild affections, rid
  In post for pleasures, bent to try
    All gamesters that would bid.
  I played with fire, did counsel spurn,
    Made life my common stake,
  But never thought that fire would burn,
    Or that a soul could ache.
  Glorious deceptions, gilded mists,
    False joys, fantastic flights,
  Pieces of sackcloth with silk-lists:

    These were my prime delights.
  I sought choice bowers, haunted the spring,
    Culled flowers and made me posies,
  Gave my fond humors their full wing,

And crowned my head with roses.
But at the height of this career
   I met with a dead man,
Who, noting well my vain abear,
   Thus unto me began:
Desist, fond fool, be not undone,
   What thou hast cut to-day
Will fade at night, and with this sun
   Quite vanish and decay.

Flowers gathered in this world die here; if thou
Wouldst have a wreath that fades not, let them grow,
And grow for thee; who spares them here shall find
A garland, where comes neither rain nor wind.

The Seed Growing Secretly

S. MARK IV. 26

If this world's friends might see but once
What some poor man may often feel,
Glory and gold and crowns and thrones
They would soon quit, and learn to kneel.

My dew, my dew, my early love,
My soul's bright food, thy absence kills!
Hover not long, eternal Dove!
Life without thee is loose, and spills.

Something I had which long ago
Did learn to suck, and sip, and taste,
But now grown sickly, sad, and slow,
Doth fret and wrangle, pine and waste.

O spread thy sacred wings and shake
One living drop! one drop life keeps!
If pious griefs heaven's joys awake,
O fill his bottle, thy child weeps!

Slowly and sadly doth he grow,
And soon as left, shrinks back to ill;
O feed that life which makes him blow
And spread and open to thy will!

For thy eternal living wells
None stained or withered shall come near;

A fresh immortal green there dwells,
And spotless white is all the wear.

Dear, secret greenness! nursed below
Tempests and winds and winter nights,
Vex not that but one sees thee grow;
That *One* made all these lesser lights.

If those bright joys he singly sheds
On thee were all met in one crown,
Both sun and stars would hide their heads,
And moons, though full, would get them down.

Let glory be their bait, whose minds
Are all too high for a low cell;
Though hawks can prey through storms and winds,
The poor bee in her hive must dwell.

Glory, the crowd's cheap tinsel still
To what most takes them, is a drudge,
And they too oft take good for ill,
And thriving vice for virtue judge.

What needs a conscience calm and bright
Within itself an outward test?

Who breaks his glass to take more light,
Makes way for storms into his rest.

Then bless thy secret growth, nor catch
At noise, but thrive unseen and dumb;
Keep clean, bear fruit, earn life, and watch
Till the white-winged reapers come!

Quickness

False life! a foil and no more, when
    Wilt thou be gone?
Thou foul deception of all men
That would not have the true come on!

Thou art a moon-like toil, a blind
    Self-posing state,
A dark contest of waves and wind,
A mere tempestuous debate.

Life is a fixed discerning light,
    A knowing joy;

No chance or fit, but ever bright
And calm and full, yet doth not cloy.

'Tis such a blissful thing, that still
   Doth vivify
And shine and smile, and hath the skill
To please without eternity.

Thou art a toilsome mole, or less,
   A moving mist;

But life is what none can express,
A quickness which my God hath kissed.

The Bird

Hither thou com'st; the busy wind all night
Blew through thy lodging, where thy own warm wing
Thy pillow was. Many a sullen storm,
For which course man seems much the fitter born,
   Rained on thy bed
   And harmless head.

And now as fresh and cheerful as the light,
Thy little heart in early hymns doth sing
Unto that Providence whose unseen arm

Curbed them, and clothed thee well and warm.
  All things that be praise him, and had
  Their lesson taught them when first made.

So hills and valleys into singing break,
And though poor stones have neither speech nor tongue,
While active winds and streams both run and speak,
Yet stones are deep in admiration.
Thus praise and prayer here beneath the sun
Make lesser mornings, when the great are done.

For each enclosèd spirit is a star,
  Enlight'ning his own little sphere,
Whose light, though fetched and borrowèd from far,
  Both mornings makes and evenings there.

But as these birds of light make a land glad,
Chirping their solemn matins on each tree,
So in the shades of night some dark fowls be,
Whose heavy notes make all that hear them sad.

The turtle then in palm trees mourns,
　　While owls and satyrs howl;
The pleasant land to brimstone turns
　　And all her streams grow foul.

Brightness and mirth, and love and faith, all fly,
Till the day-spring breaks forth again from high.

The Waterfall

With what deep murmurs through time's silent stealth
Doth thy transparent, cool, and wat'ry wealth
　　　Here flowing fall,
　　　And chide, and call,
As if his liquid, loose retínue stayed
Ling'ring, and were of this steep place afraid,
　　　The common pass
　　　Where, clear as glass,
　　　All must descend—
　　　Not to an end,
But quickened by this deep and rocky grave,
Rise to a longer course more bright and brave.

　Dear stream! dear bank, where often I
　Have sat and pleased my pensive eye,
　Why, since each drop of thy quick store
　Runs thither whence it flowed before,
　Should poor souls fear a shade or night,
　Who came, sure, from a sea of light?
　Or since those drops are all sent back
　So sure to thee, that none doth lack,
　Why should frail flesh doubt any more
　That what God takes he'll not restore?

　O useful element and clear!
　My sacred wash and cleanser here,
　My first consigner unto those
　Fountains of life where the Lamb goes!
　What sublime truths and wholesome themes
　Lodge in thy mystical deep streams!
　Such as dull man can never find
　Unless that spirit lead his mind
　Which first upon thy face did move,

And hatched all with his quick'ning love.
As this loud brook's incessant fall
In streaming rings restagnates all,
Which reach by course the bank, and then
Are no more seen, just so pass men.
O my invisible estate,
My glorious liberty, still late!
Thou art the channel my soul seeks,
Not this with cataracts and creeks.

Man

Weighing the steadfastness and state
Of some mean things which here below reside,
Where birds like watchful clocks the noiseless date
    And intercourse of times divide,
Where bees at night get home and hive, and flowers
        Early, as well as late,
Rise with the sun, and set in the same bowers;

I would, said I, my God would give
The staidness of these things to man! for these
To his divine appointments ever cleave,
    And no new business breaks their peace;
The birds nor sow nor reap, yet sup and dine,
        The flowers without clothes live,
Yet Solomon was never dressed so fine.

Man hath still either toys or care,
He hath no root, nor to one place is tied,
But ever restless and irregular
    About this earth doth run and ride;
He knows he hath a home, but scarce knows where,
        He says it is so far
That he hath quite forgot how to go there.

He knocks at all the doors, strays and roams,
Nay, hath not so much wit as some stones have,
Which in the darkest nights point to their homes
    By some hid sense their maker gave;
Man is the shuttle, to whose winding quest
        And passage through these looms
God ordered motion, but ordained no rest.

The Night

JOHN III. 2

> Through that pure virgin-shrine,
> That sacred veil drawn o'er thy glorious noon,
> That men might look and live, as glow-worms shine,
>   And face the moon,
>   Wise Nicodemus saw such light
>   As made him know his God by night.
>
>   Most blest believer he!
> Who in that land of darkness and blind eyes
> Thy long-expected healing wings could see
>   When thou didst rise,
>   And what can never more be done,
>   Did at midnight speak with the Sun!
>
>   Oh, who will tell me where
> He found thee at that dead and silent hour!
> What hallowed solitary ground did bear
>   So rare a flower,
>   Within whose sacred leaves did lie
>   The fullness of the deity.
>
>   No mercy-seat of gold,
> No dead and dusty cherub, nor carved stone,
> But his own living works did my Lord hold
>   And lodge alone,
> Where trees and herbs did watch and peep
> And wonder, while the Jews did sleep.
>
>   Dear night! this world's defeat;
> The stop to busy fools; care's check and curb;
> The day of spirits; my soul's calm retreat
>   Which none disturb;
>   Christ's progress, and his prayer time;
>   The hours to which high heaven doth chime;
>
>   God's silent, searching flight;
> When my Lord's head is filled with dew, and all
> His locks are wet with the clear drops of night;
>   His still, soft call;
>   His knocking time; the soul's dumb watch,
>   When spirits their fair kindred catch.

Were all my loud, evil days
Calm and unhaunted as is thy dark tent,
Whose peace but by some angel's wing or voice
    Is seldom rent,
  Then I in heaven all the long year
  Would keep, and never wander here.

  But living where the sun
Doth all things wake, and where all mix and tire
Themselves and others, I consent and run
    To ev'ry mire,
  And by this world's ill-guiding light,
  Err more than I can do by night.

  There is in God, some say,
A deep but dazzling darkness, as men here
Say it is late and dusky, because they
    See not all clear;
  Oh, for that night, where I in him
  Might live invisible and dim!

The Search

'Tis now clear day: I see a rose
Bud in the bright east, and disclose
The pilgrim-sun. All night have I
Spent in a roving ecstasy
To find my Savior; I have been
As far as Bethlem, and have seen
His inn and cradle; being there
I met the wise men, asked them where
He might be found, or what star can
Now point him out, grown up a man.
To Egypt hence I fled, ran o'er
All her parched bosom to Nile's shore,
Her yearly nurse; came back, inquired
Amongst the doctors, and desired
To see the temple, but was shown
A little dust, and for the town
A heap of ashes, where some said
A small bright sparkle was a bed
Which would one day, beneath the pole,

Awake, and then refine the whole.
  Tired here, I came to Sychar; thence
To Jacob's well, bequeathëd since
Unto his sons, where often they
In those calm golden evenings lay,
Wat'ring their flocks, and having spent
Those white days, drove home to the tent
Their well-fleeced train. And here, O fate,
I sit, where once my Savior sate;
The angry spring in bubbles swelled
Which broke in sighs still, as they filled
And whispered, Jesus had been there,
But Jacob's children would not hear.
Loath hence to part, at last I rise
But with the fountain in my eyes,
And here a fresh search is decreed,
He must be found where he did bleed;
I walk the garden, and there see
Ideas of his agony,
And moving anguishments that set
His blest face in a bloody sweat;
I climbed the hill, perused the cross
Hung with my gain and his great loss;
Never did tree bear fruit like this,
Balsam of souls, the body's bliss.
But oh, his grave! where I saw lent,
For he had none, a monument,
An undefiled and new-hewed one,
But there was not the corner-stone;
Sure, then said I, my quest is vain,
He'll not be found where he was slain;
So mild a Lamb can never be
'Midst so much blood and cruelty.
I'll to the wilderness, and can
Find beasts more merciful than man;
He lived there safe, 'twas his retreat
From the fierce Jew, and Herod's heat,
And forty days withstood the fell
And high temptatïons of hell;
With seraphins there talkëd he,
His father's flaming ministry;
He heaven'd their walks, and with his eyes

Made those wild shades a paradise,
Thus was the desert sanctified
To be the refuge of his bride;
I'll thither then; see, it is day,
The sun's broke through to guide my way.
   But as I urged thus, and writ down
What pleasures should my journey crown,
What silent paths, what shades and cells,
Fair virgin-flowers, and hallowed wells,
I should rove in, and rest my head
Where my dear Lord did often tread,
Sug'ring all dangers with success,
Methought I heard one singing thus:

      Leave, leave thy gadding thoughts;
          Who pores
          And spies
       Still out of doors,
          Descries
      Within them nought.

     The skin and shell of things,
         Though fair,
          Are not
        Thy wish nor prayer,
          But got
       By mere despair
          Of wings.

    To rack old elements,
          Or dust,
         And say

    Sure here he must
         Needs stay,
     Is not the way,
         Nor just.
Search well another world: who studies this,
Travels in clouds, seeks manna where none is.

Regeneration

   A ward, and still in bonds, one day
      I stole abroad;
  It was high spring, and all the way

Primrosed and hung with shade;
  Yet was it frost within,
      And surly winds
Blasted my infant buds, and sin
  Like clouds eclipsed my mind.

Stormed thus, I straight perceived my spring
      Mere stage and show,
My walk a monstrous mountained thing,
  Rough-cast with rocks and snow;
    And as a pilgrim's eye,
        Far from relief,
Measures the melancholy sky,
  Then drops and rains for grief,

So sighed I upwards still; at last
      'Twixt steps and falls
I reached the pinnacle, where placed
  I found a pair of scales;
    I took them up and laid
        In th' one, late pains;
The other smoke and pleasures weighed,
  But proved the heavier grains.

With that some cried, Away!
        Straight I
        Obeyed, and led
Full east, a fair, fresh field could spy;
  Some called it Jacob's bed,
    A virgin soil which no
        Rude feet ere trod,
Where, since he stepped there, only go
        Prophets and Friends of God.

Here I reposed; but scarce well set,
        A grove descried
Of stately height, whose branches met
    And mixed on every side;
      I entered, and once in,
          Amazed to see't,
Found all was changed, and a new spring
    Did all my senses greet.
The unthrift sun shot vital gold,
      A thousand pieces,

And heaven its azure did unfold,
   Checkered with snowy fleeces;
   The air was all in spice,
      And every bush
A garland wore; thus fed my eyes,
   But all the ear lay hush.

Only a little fountain lent
   Some use for ears,
And on the dumb shades language spent,
   The music of her tears;
   I drew her near, and found
      The cistern full
Of divers stones, some bright and round,
   Others ill-shaped and dull.

The first, pray mark, as quick as light
   Danced through the flood,
But th' last, more heavy than the night,
   Nailed to the center stood;
   I wondered much, but tired
      At last with thought,
My restless eye that still desired
   As strange an object brought.

It was a bank of flowers, where I descried,
   Though 'twas mid-day,
Some fast asleep, others broad- eyed
   And taking in the ray;
   Here musing long, I heard
      A rushing wind

Which still increased, but whence it stirred
   No where I could not find.

I turned me round, and to each shade
   Dispatched an eye
To see if any leaf had made
   Least motion or reply,
   But while I list'ning sought
      My mind to ease
By knowing where 'twas, or where not,
   It whispered: Where I please.

Lord, then said I, on me one breath,
And let me die before my death!

The Dwelling-Place

S. JOHN I. 38–39

What happy secret fountain,
  Fair shade or mountain,
Whose undiscovered virgin glory
Boasts it this day, though not in story,
Was then thy dwelling? Did some cloud,
Fixed to a tent, descend and shroud
My distressed Lord? Or did a star,
Beckoned by thee, though high and far,
In sparkling smiles haste gladly down
To lodge light and increase her own?
My dear, dear God! I do not know
What lodged thee then, nor where, nor how;
But I am sure thou dost now come
Oft to a narrow, homely room,
Where thou too hast but the least part,
My God, I mean my sinful heart.

The Retreat

Happy those early days when I
Shined in my angel-infancy!
Before I understood this place
Appointed for my second race,
Or taught my soul to fancy aught
But a white celestial thought;
When yet I had not walked above

A mile or two from my first love,
And looking back at that short space,
Could see a glimpse of his bright face;
When on some gilded cloud or flower
My gazing soul would dwell an hour,
And in those weaker glories spy
Some shadows of eternity;
Before I taught my tongue to wound
My conscience with a sinful sound,
Or had the black art to dispense
A sev'ral sin to ev'ry sense;
But felt through all this fleshly dress
Bright shoots of everlastingness.
    Oh, how I long to travel back

And tread again that ancient track!
That I might once more reach that plain
Where first I left my glorious train,
From whence th' enlightened spirit sees
That shady city of palm trees.
But, ah, my soul with too much stay
Is drunk, and staggers in the way.
Some men a forward motion love,
But I by backward steps would move,
And when this dust falls to the urn,
In that state I came, return.

Childhood

I cannot reach it, and my striving eye
Dazzles at it, as at eternity.
  Were now that chronicle alive,
Those white designs which children drive,
And the thoughts of each harmless hour,
With their content too in my power,
Quickly would I make my path even,
And by mere playing go to heaven.

  Why should men love
A wolf more than a lamb or dove?
Or choose hell-fire and brimstone streams
Before bright stars and God's own beams?
Who kisseth thorns will hurt his face,
But flowers do both refresh and grace,
And sweetly living (fie on men!)

Are when dead, medicinal then.
If seeing much should make staid eyes,

And long experience should make wise,
Since all that age doth teach is ill,
Why should I not love childhood still?
Why if I see a rock or shelf,
Shall I from thence cast down myself,
Or by complying with the world,
From the same precipice be hurled?
Those observations are but foul
Which make me wise to lose my soul.

And yet the practicing worldlings call
Business and weighty action all,

Checking the poor child for his play,
But gravely cast themselves away.

Dear, harmless age! the short, swift span
Where weeping virtue parts with man;
Where love without lust dwells, and bends
What way we please, without self-ends.

An age of mysteries! which he
Must live twice, that would God's face see;
Which angels guard, and with it play;
Angels, which foul men drive away!

How do I study now and scan
Thee, more than ere I studied man,
And only see through a long night
Thy edges, and thy bordering light!
Oh, for thy center and mid-day!
For sure that is the narrow way.

The Dawning

Ah! what time wilt thou come? when shall that cry,
The bridegroom's coming, fill the sky?
Shall it in the evening run,
When our words and works are done?
Or will thy all-surprising light
　　　Break at midnight?
When either sleep or some dark pleasure
Possesseth mad man without measure,
Or shall these early fragrant hours
　　　Unlock thy bowers?
And with their blush of light descry
Thy locks crowned with eternity?
Indeed, it is the only time
That with thy glory doth best chime;
All now are stirring, ev'ry field
　　　Full hymns doth yield,
The whole creation shakes off night,
And for thy shadow looks the light;
Stars now vanish without number,
Sleepy planets set and slumber,
The pursy clouds disband and scatter,
All expect some sudden matter;

Not one beam triumphs, but from far
    That morning star.
Oh, at what time soever thou,
Unknown to us, the heaven wilt bow,
And with thy angels in the van
Descend to judge poor careless man,
Grant I may not like puddle lie
In a corrupt security,
Where, if a traveler water crave,
He finds it dead and in a grave;
But as this restless vocal spring
All day and night doth run and sing,
And though here born, yet is acquainted
Elsewhere, and flowing keeps untainted,
So let me all my busy age
In thy free services engage;
And though while here of force I must
Have commerce sometimes with poor dust,
And in my flesh, though vile and low,
As this doth in her channel flow,
Yet let my course, my aim, my love,
And chief acquaintance be above;
So when that day and hour shall come
In which thyself will be the sun,
Thou'lt find me dressed and on my way,
Watching the break of thy great day.

The Morning Watch

O joys! infinite sweetness! with what flowers
And shoots of glory my soul breaks and buds!
    All the long hours
    Of night and rest,
    Through the still shrouds
    Of sleep and clouds,
  This dew fell on my breast;
    Oh, how it bloods
And spirits all my earth! Hark! in what rings
And hymning circulations the quick world

    Awakes and sings;
    The rising winds
    And falling springs,

Birds, beasts, all things
Adore him in their kinds.
Thus all is hurled
In sacred hymns and order, the great chime
And symphony of nature. Prayer is
The world in tune,
A spirit voice,
And vocal joys
Whose echo is heav'n's bliss.
O let me climb

When I lie down! The pious soul by night
Is like a clouded star whose beams, though said
To shed their light
Under some cloud,
Yet are above,
And shine and move
Beyond that misty shroud.
So in my bed,
That curtained grave, though sleep like ashes hide
My lamp and life, both shall in thee abide.

The World

I saw eternity the other night
Like a great ring of pure and endless light,
All calm as it was bright;
And round beneath it, time in hours, days, years,
Driv'n by the spheres,

Like a vast shadow moved, in which the world
And all her train were hurled:
The doting lover in his quaintest strain
Did there complain;
Near him his lute, his fancy, and his flights,
Wit's sour delights,
With gloves and knots, the silly snares of pleasure,
Yet his dear treasure,
All scattered lay, while he his eyes did pore
Upon a flower.

The darksome statesman, hung with weights and woe,
Like a thick midnight fog moved there so slow
He did not stay, nor go;

Condemning thoughts, like sad eclipses, scowl
          Upon his soul,
And clouds of crying witnesses without
          Pursued him with one shout;
Yet digged the mole, and lest his ways be found
          Worked underground,
Where he did clutch his prey, but One did see
          That policy;
Churches and altars fed him; perjuries
          Were gnats and flies;
          It rained about him blood and tears, but he
          Drank them as free.

The fearful miser on a heap of rust
Sat pining all his life there, did scarce trust
          His own hands with the dust,
Yet would not place one piece above, but lives
          In fear of thieves.
Thousands there were as frantic as himself,
          And hugged each one his pelf:
The downright epicure placed heav'n in sense,
          And scorned pretense;
While others, slipped into a wide excess,
          Said little less;
The weaker sort slight trivial wares enslave,
          Who think them brave;
And poor despisèd truth sat counting by
          Their victory.

Yet some, who all this while did weep and sing,
And sing and weep, soared up into the ring;
          But most would use no wing.
O fools, said I, thus to prefer dark night
          Before true light,
To live in grots and caves, and hate the day
          Because it shows the way,
The way which from this dead and dark abode
          Leads up to God,
A way where you might tread the sun, and be
          More bright than he.
But as I did their madness so discuss,
          One whispered thus:
This ring the bridegroom did for none provide
          But for his bride.

Ascension Hymn

Dust and clay,
Man's ancient wear!
Here must you stay,
But I elsewhere;
Souls sojourn here, but may not rest;
Who will ascend must be undressed.

And yet some
That know to die
Before death come,
Walk to the sky
Even in this life; but all such can
Leave behind them the old man.

If a star
Should leave the sphere,
She must first mar
Her flaming wear,
And after fall, for in her dress
Of glory she cannot transgress.

Man of old
Within the line
Of Eden could,
Like the sun, shine
All naked, innocent and bright,
And intimate with heav'n as light;

But since he
That brightness soiled,
His garments be
All dark and spoiled,
And here are left as nothing worth,
Till the refiner's fire breaks forth.

Then comes he!
Whose mighty light
Made his clothes be,
Like heav'n, all bright—
The Fuller whose pure blood did flow
To make stained man more white than snow.

He alone,
And none else, can

> Bring bone to bone
> And rebuild man,
> And by his all-subduing might,
> Make clay ascend more quick than light.

They Are All Gone Into the World of Light

They are all gone into the world of light!
   And I alone sit lingering here;
Their very memory is fair and bright,
   And my sad thoughts doth clear.

It glows and glitters in my cloudy breast
   Like stars upon some gloomy grove,
Or those faint beams in which this hill is dressed
   After the sun's remove.

I see them walking in an air of glory,
   Whose light doth trample on my days,
My days, which are at best but dull and hoary,
   Mere glimmering and decays.

O holy hope and high humility,
   High as the heavens above!
These are your walks, and you have showed them me
   To kindle my cold love.

Dear, beauteous death! the jewel of the just!
   Shining no where but in the dark;
What mysteries do lie beyond thy dust,
   Could man outlook that mark!

He that hath found some fledged bird's nest may know
   At first sight if the bird be flown;
But what fair well or grove he sings in now,
   That is to him unknown.

And yet, as angels in some brighter dreams
   Call to the soul when man doth sleep,
So some strange thoughts transcend our wonted themes,
   And into glory peep.

If a star were confined into a tomb,
   Her captive flames must needs burn there;
But when the hand that locked her up gives room,
   She'll shine through all the sphere.

O Father of eternal life, and all
    Created glories under thee,
Resume thy spirit from this world of thrall
    Into true liberty!

Either disperse these mists which blot and fill
    My perspective, still, as they pass,
Or else remove me hence unto that hill
    Where I shall need no glass.

Unprofitableness

How rich, O Lord, how fresh thy visits are!
'Twas but just now my bleak leaves hopeless hung,
    Sullied with dust and mud;
Each snarling blast shot through me, and did share
Their youth and beauty; cold showers nipped and wrung
    Their spiciness and blood;
But since thou didst in one sweet glance survey
Their sad decays, I flourish, and once more
    Breathe all perfumes and spice;
I smell a dew like myrrh, and all the day
Wear in my bosom a full sun; such store
    Hath one beam from thy eyes.
But ah, my God, what fruit hast thou of this?
What one poor leaf did ever I let fall
    To wait upon thy wreath?
Thus thou all day a thankless weed dost dress,
And when th' hast done, a stench or fog is all
    The odor I bequeath.

Peace

    My soul, there is a country
        Far beyond the stars,
    Where stands a wingéd sentry
        A skillful in the wars;
    There above noise and danger
      Sweet peace sits crowned with smiles,
    And one born in a manger
        Commands the beauteous files;
    He is thy gracious friend,
        And (O my soul, awake!)

Did in pure love descend
    To die here for thy sake.
If thou canst get but thither,
    There grows the flower of peace,
The rose that cannot wither,
    Thy fortress and thy ease;
Leave then thy foolish ranges,
    For none can thee secure
But one who never changes,
    Thy God, thy life, thy cure.

THOMAS TRAHERNE (1637–1674)

Considered the last of the metaphysical poets, Traherne, the son of a
poor shoemaker, was educated at Oxford and ordained an Anglican
clergyman in 1660. Most of his poetry was lost until 1896, when two
of his manuscripts were discovered by chance in London. These were
published as *Poetical Works* in 1903, and *Centuries of Meditations* in
1908. Like the poetry of Blake and Whitman, Traherne's work explores
the themes of loss of childhood innocence and the failure of adults
to appreciate the beauty and divinity of creation. For Traherne, true
felicity—in poetry as in life—was to be found in the imitation of the
child's untutored joy in the natural things of the world.

Wonder

How like an angel came I down!
    How bright are all things here!
When first among his works I did appear,
    Oh, how their glory did me crown!
The world resembled his eternity,
        In which my soul did walk;
    And ev'rything that I did see
        Did with me talk.

The skies in their magnificence,
    The lovely lively air,
Oh, how divine, how soft, how sweet, how fair!
    The stars did entertain my sense,
And all the works of God so bright and pure,
        So rich and great, did seem,

As if they ever must endure
        In my esteem.

A native health and innocence
        Within my bones did grow,
And while my God did all his glories show,
        I felt a vigor in my sense
That was all spirit; I within did flow
        With seas of life like wine;
        I nothing in the world did know,
        But 'twas divine.

Harsh rugged objects were concealed;
        Oppressions, tears, and cries,
Sins, griefs, complaints, dissensions, weeping eyes,
        Were hid, and only things revealed
Which heavenly spirits and the angels prize:
        The state of innocence
        And bliss, not trades and poverties,
        Did fill my sense.

The streets seemed paved with golden stones,
        The boys and girls all mine—
To me how did their lovely faces shine!
        The sons of men all holy ones,
In joy and beauty then appeared to me;
        And ev'rything I found,
        While like an angel I did see,
        Adorned the ground.

Rich diamonds, and pearl, and gold
        Might ev'rywhere be seen;
Rare colors, yellow, blue, red, white, and green,
        Mine eyes on ev'ry side behold;
All that I saw a wonder did appear,
        Amazement was my bliss,
        That and my wealth met ev'rywhere;
        No joy to this!

Cursed, ill-devised proprieties,
        With envy, avarice,
And fraud, those fiends that spoil ev'n paradise,
        Were not the object of mine eyes;
Nor hedges, ditches, limits, narrow bounds,

I dreamt not aught of those,
But in surveying all men's grounds
I found repose.

For property itself was mine,
And hedges, ornaments,
Walls, houses, coffers, and their rich contents,
To make me rich combine.
Clothes, costly jewels, laces, I esteemed
My wealth, by others worn,
For me they all to wear them seemed,
When I was born.

Eden

A learned and happy ignorance
Divided me
From all the vanity,
From all the sloth, care, sorrow, that advance
The madness and the misery
Of men. No error, no distraction, I
Saw cloud the earth, or overcast the sky.

I knew not that there was a serpent's sting,
Whose poison shed
On men did overspread
The world, nor did I dream of such a thing
As sin, in which mankind lay dead.

They all were brisk and living things to me,
Yea, pure and full of immortality.

Joy, pleasure, beauty, kindness, charming love,
Sleep, life, and light,
Peace, melody—my sight,
Mine ears, and heart did fill and freely move;
All that I saw did me delight;
The universe was then a world of treasure,
To me an universal world of pleasure.

Unwelcome penitence I then thought not on;
Vain costly toys,
Swearing and roaring boys,
Shops, markets, taverns, coaches, were unknown,
So all things were that drown my joys;

No thorns choked up my path, nor hid the face
Of bliss and glory, nor eclipsed my place.

Only what Adam in his first estate,
           Did I behold;
        Hard silver and dry gold
As yet lay underground; my happy fate
      Was more acquainted with the old
And innocent delights which he did see
In his original simplicity.

Those things which first his Eden did adorn,
           My infancy
        Did crown; simplicity
Was my protection when I first was born.
      Mine eyes those treasures first did see
Which God first made; the first effects of love
My first enjoyments upon earth did prove,

And were so great, and so divine, so pure,
           So fair and sweet,
        So true, when I did meet
Them here at first they did my soul allure,
      And drew away mine infant feet
Quite from the works of men, that I might see
The glorious wonders of the Deity.

News

      News from a foreign country came,
As if my treasures and my joys lay there;
      So much it did my heart inflame,
'Twas wont to call my soul into mine ear,
        Which thither went to meet
           Th' approaching sweet,
        And on the threshold stood
To entertain the secret good;
        It hovered there
        As if 'twould leave mine ear,
     And was so eager to embrace
Th' expected tidings as they came,
That it could change its dwelling place
        To meet the voice of fame;

As if new tidings were the things
Which did comprise my wishëd unknown treasure,
Or else did bear them on their wings,
With so much joy they came, with so much pleasure.
My soul stood at the gate
To recreate
Itself with bliss, and woo
Its speedier approach; a fuller view
It fain would take,
Yet journeys back would make
Unto my heart, as if 'twould fain
Go out to meet, yet stay within,
Fitting a place to entertain
And bring the tidings in.

What sacred instinct did inspire
My soul in childhood with an hope so strong?
What secret force moved my desire
T' expect my joys beyond the seas, so young?
Felicity I knew
Was out of view;
And being left alone,
I thought all happiness was gone
From earth; for this

I longed for absent bliss,
Deeming that sure beyond the seas,
Or else in something near at hand
Which I knew not, since nought did please
I knew, my bliss did stand.

But little did the infant dream
That all the treasures of the world were by,
And that himself was so the cream
And crown of all which round about did lie.
Yet thus it was! The gem,
The diadem,
The ring enclosing all
That stood upon this earthen ball,
The heav'nly eye,
Much wider than the sky,

Wherein they all included were,
The love, the soul, that was the king
Made to possess them, did appear
    A very little thing.

The Apostasy

One star
Is better far
Than many precious stones;
One sun, which is by its own luster seen,
    Is worth ten thousand golden thrones;
    A juicy herb, or spire of grass,
    In useful virtue, native green,
        An em'rald doth surpass,
    Hath in 't more value, though less seen.

No wars,
Nor mortal jars,
Nor bloody feuds, nor coin,
Nor griefs which those occasion, saw I then;
    Nor wicked thieves which this purloin;
    I had no thoughts that were impure;
    Esteeming both women and men
        God's work, I was secure,
    And reckoned peace my choicest gem.

As Eve,
I did believe
Myself in Eden set,
Affecting neither gold nor ermined crowns,
    Nor aught else that I need forget;
    No mud did foul my limpid streams,
    No mist eclipsed my sun with frowns;
        Set off with heav'nly beams,
    My joys were meadows, fields, and towns.

Those things
Which cherubins
Did not at first behold
Among God's works, which Adam did not see—
    As robes, and stones enchased in gold,

Rich cabinets, and such-like fine
Inventions—could not ravish me;
   I thought not bowls of wine
Needful for my felicity.

     All bliss
   Consists in this,
  To do as Adam did,
And not to know those superficial joys
   Which were from him in Eden hid,
   Those little new-invented things,
   Fine lace and silks, such childish toys
    As ribands are and rings,
  Or worldly pelf that us destroys.

     For God,
   Both great and good,
  The seeds of melancholy
Created not, but only foolish men,
   Grown mad with customary folly
   Which doth increase their wants, so dote
  As when they elder grow they then
    Such baubles chiefly note;
  More fools at twenty years than ten.

     But I,
   I know not why,
  Did learn among them too,
At length; and when I once with blemished eyes
   Began their pence and toys to view,
  Drowned in their customs, I became
  A stranger to the shining skies,

   Lost as a dying flame,
  And hobby-horses brought to prize.

    The sun
  And moon forgone
  As if unmade, appear
No more to me; to God and heaven dead
   I was, as though they never were;
   Upon some useless gaudy book,
  When what I knew of God was fled,

The child being taught to look,
His soul was quickly murtherëd.

O fine!
O most divine!
O brave! they cried; and showed
Some tinsel thing whose glittering did amaze,
And to their cries its beauty owed:
Thus I on riches, by degrees,
Of a new stamp did learn to gaze,
While all the world for these
I lost, my joy turned to a blaze.

Poverty

As in the house I sate,
Alone and desolate,
No creature but the fire and I,
The chimney and the stool, I lift mine eye
Up to the wall,
And in the silent hall
Saw nothing mine
But some few cups and dishes shine,
The table and the wooden stools
Where people used to dine;
A painted cloth there was,
Wherein some ancient story wrought
A little entertained my thought,
Which light discovered through the glass.

I wondered much to see
That all my wealth should be
Confined in such a little room,
Yet hope for more I scarcely durst presume.
It grieved me sore
That such a scanty store
Should be my all;
For I forgot my ease and health,
Nor did I think of hands or eyes,
Nor soul nor body prize;
I neither thought the sun,
Nor moon, nor stars, nor people, mine,
Though they did round about me shine;
And therefore was I quite undone.

Some greater things, I thought,
Must needs for me be wrought,
Which till my craving mind could see
I ever should lament my poverty;
I fain would have
Whatever bounty gave,
Nor could there be
Without or love or deity;
For should not he be infinite
Whose hand created me?
Ten thousand absent things
Did vex my poor and wanting mind,
Which, till I be no longer blind,
Let me not see the King of kings.

His love must surely be
Rich, infinite, and free;
Nor can he be thought a God
Of grace and power, that fills not his abode,
His holy court,
In kind and liberal sort;
Joys and pleasures,
Plenty of jewels, goods, and treasures,
To enrich the poor, cheer the forlorn,
His palace must adorn,
And given all to me;
For till his works my wealth became,
No love or peace did me inflame:
But now I have a Deity.

Right Apprehension

Give but to things their true esteem,
And those which now so vile and worthless seem
Will so much fill and please the mind
That we shall there the only riches find.
How wise was I
In infancy!
I then saw in the clearest light;
But corrupt custom is a second night.

Custom, that must a trophy be
When wisdom shall complete her victory;
For trades, opinions, errors, are

False lights, but yet received to set off ware
        More false; we're sold
        For worthless gold.
        Diana was a goddess made
That silversmiths might have the better trade.

        But give to things their true esteem,
And then what's magnified most vile will seem;
        What commonly's despised will be
The truest and the greatest rarity.
        What men should prize
        They all despise:
        The best enjoyments are abused;
The only wealth by madmen is refused.

        A globe of earth is better far
Than if it were a globe of gold; a star
        Much brighter than a precious stone;
The sun more glorious than a costly throne—
        His warming beam,
        A living stream
        Of liquid pearl, that from a spring
Waters the earth, is a most precious thing.

        What newness once suggested to,
Now clearer reason doth improve my view;
        By novelty my soul was taught
At first, but now reality my thought
        Inspires; and I
        Perspicuously
        Each way instructed am by sense,
Experience, reason, and intelligence.

        A globe of gold must barren be,
Untilled and useless; we should neither see
        Trees, flowers, grass, or corn
Such a metalline massy globe adorn;
        As splendor blinds
        So hardness binds,
        No fruitfulness it can produce;
A golden world can't be of any use.

        Ah me! this world is more divine;
The wisdom of a god in this doth shine.
        What ails mankind to be so cross?

The useful earth they count vile dirt and dross,
        And neither prize
        Its qualities
    Nor donor's love. I fain would know
How or why men God's goodness disallow.

      The earth's rare ductile soil,
Which duly yields unto the plowman's toil
      Its fertile nature, gives offence,
And its improvement by the influence
        Of heav'n; for these
        Do not well please,
Because they do upbraid men's hardened hearts,
And each of them an evidence imparts

      Against the owner; whose design
It is that nothing be reputed fine,
      Nor held for any excellence
Of which he hath not in himself the sense.
        He too well knows
        That no fruit grows
    In him, obdurate wretch, who yields
Obedience to heav'n less than the fields.

      But being, like his lovèd gold,
Stiff, barren, and impen'trable, though told
      He should be otherwise, he is
Uncapable of any heav'nly bliss.
        His gold and he
        Do well agree,
      For he's a formal hypocrite,
Like that, unfruitful, yet on th' outside bright.

      Ah, happy infant! wealthy heir!
How blessed did the heaven and earth appear
      Before thou knew'st there was a thing
Called gold! barren of good, of ill the spring
        Beyond compare!
        Most quiet were
Those infant days when I did see
Wisdom and wealth couched in simplicity.

The Rapture

Sweet infancy!
O heavenly fire! O sacred light!
How fair and bright!
How great am I,
Whom the whole world doth magnify!

O heavenly joy!
O great and sacred blessedness
Which I possess!
So great a joy
Who did into my arms convey?

From God above
Being sent, the gift doth me inflame
To praise his name;
The stars do move,
The sun doth shine, to show his love.

Oh, how divine
Am I! To all this sacred
wealth,
This life and health,
Who raised? who mine
Did make the same? what hand divine?

Felicity

Prompted to seek my bliss above the skies,
How often did I lift mine eyes
Beyond the spheres!
Dame Nature told me there was endless space
Within my soul; I spied its very face.
Sure it not for nought appears;
What is there which a man may see
Beyond the spheres?
Felicity.

There in the mind of God, that sphere of love,
In nature, height, extent, above
All other spheres,
A man may see himself, the world, the bride
Of God, his church, which as they there are eyed,
Strangely exalted each appears;
His mind is higher than the space
Above the spheres,
Surmounts all place.

No empty space—it is all full of sight,
    All soul and life, an eye most bright,
      All light and love,
Which doth at once all things possess and give,
Heaven and earth, with all that therein live;
    It rests at quiet, and doth move;
    Eternal is, yet time includes;
      A scene above
      All interludes.

Dreams

    'Tis strange! I saw the skies,
I saw the hills before mine eyes,
      The sparrow fly,
The lands that did about me lie,
The real sun, that heavenly eye!
Can closèd eyes ev'n in the darkest night
See through their lids, and be informed with sight?

    The people were to me
    As true as those by day I see,
      As true the air;
    The earth as sweet, as fresh, as fair,
    As that which did by day repair
Unto my waking sense! Can all the sky,
Can all the world, within my brain-pan lie?

    What sacred secret's this
    Which seems to intimate my bliss?
      What is there in
    The narrow confines of my skin
    That is alive, and feels within
When I am dead? Can magnitude possess
An active memory, yet not be less?

    May all that I can see
    Awake, by night within me be?
      My childhood knew
    No difference, but all was true,
    As real all as what I view;
The world itself was there; 'twas wondrous strange
That heav'n and earth should so their place exchange.

    Till that which vulgar sense
    Doth falsely call experience

Distinguished things,
The ribands, and the gaudy wings
Of birds, the virtues and the sins,
That represented were in dreams by night,
As really my senses did delight.

Or grieve, as those I saw
By day; things terrible did awe
My soul with fear;
The apparitions seemed as near
As things could be, and things they were;
Yet were they all by fancy in me wrought,
And all their being founded in a thought.

Oh, what a thing is thought!
Which seems a dream, yea, seemeth nought,
Yet doth the mind
Affect as much as what we find
Most near and true! Sure men are blind,
And can't the forcible reality
Of things that secret are within them see.

Thought! Surely thoughts are true;
They please as much as things can do;
Nay, things are dead,
And in themselves are severëd
From souls; nor can they fill the head
Without our thoughts. Thoughts are the real things
From whence all joy, from whence all sorrow springs.

Insatiableness

This busy, vast, inquiring soul
Brooks no control,
No limits will endure,
Nor any rest; it will all see,
Not time alone, but ev'n eternity.
What is it? Endless, sure.

'Tis mean ambition to desire
A single world;
To many I aspire,
Though one upon another hurled;
Nor will they all, if they be all confined,
Delight my mind.

This busy, vast, inquiring soul
Brooks no control;

'Tis very curious too.
        Each one of all those worlds must be
Enriched with infinite variety
        And worth, or 'twill not do.

        'Tis nor delight nor perfect pleasure
                To have a purse
        That hath a bottom in its treasure,
Since I must thence endless expense disburse.
Sure there's a God, for else there's no delight,
                One infinite.

The Review

        Did I grow? or did I stay?
        Did I prosper or decay,
                When I so
        From things to thoughts did go?
Did I flourish or diminish,
When I so in thoughts did finish
What I had in things begun;
When from God's works to think upon
The thoughts of men my soul did come?
The thoughts of men, had they been wise,
Should more delight me than the skies;
                They mighty creatures are,
                        For these the mind
Affect, afflict, do ease or grind;
                But foolish thoughts ensnare.

        Wise ones are a sacred treasure;
        True ones yield substantial pleasure;
                Compared to them,
                I things as shades esteem.
False ones are a foolish flourish,
Such as mortals chiefly nourish;
When I them to things compare,
Compared to things, they trifles are;
Bad thoughts do hurt, deceive, ensnare;
A good man's thoughts are of such price
That they create a paradise;
                But he that misemploys
                        That faculty,
God, men, and angels doth defy,
                Robs them of all their joys.

Index of Titles

Index of First Lines

DOVER · THRIFT · EDITIONS

POETRY

LA VITA NUOVA, Dante Alighieri. 56pp. 0-486-41915-0

101 GREAT AMERICAN POEMS, The American Poetry & Literacy Project (ed.). (Available in U.S. only.) 96pp. 0-486-40158-8

ENGLISH ROMANTIC POETRY: An Anthology, Stanley Appelbaum (ed.). 256pp. 0-486-29282-7

BHAGAVADGITA, Bhagavadgita. 112pp. 0-486-27782-8

THE BOOK OF PSALMS, King James Bible. 128pp. 0-486-27541-8

IMAGIST POETRY: AN ANTHOLOGY, Bob Blaisdell (ed.). 176pp. (Available in U.S. only.) 0-486-40875-2

BLAKE'S SELECTED POEMS, William Blake. 96pp. 0-486-28517-0

SONGS OF INNOCENCE AND SONGS OF EXPERIENCE, William Blake. 64pp. 0-486-27051-3

THE CLASSIC TRADITION OF HAIKU: An Anthology, Faubion Bowers (ed.). 96pp. 0-486-29274-6

TO MY HUSBAND AND OTHER POEMS, Anne Bradstreet (Robert Hutchinson, ed.). 80pp. 0-486-41408-6

BEST POEMS OF THE BRONTË SISTERS (ed. by Candace Ward), Emily, Anne, and Charlotte Brontë: 64pp. 0-486-29529-X

SONNETS FROM THE PORTUGUESE AND OTHER POEMS, Elizabeth Barrett Browning. 64pp. 0-486-27052-1

MY LAST DUCHESS AND OTHER POEMS, Robert Browning. 128pp. 0-486-27783-6

POEMS AND SONGS, Robert Burns. 96pp. 0-486-26863-2

SELECTED POEMS, George Gordon, Lord Byron. 112pp. 0-486-27784-4

JABBERWOCKY AND OTHER POEMS, Lewis Carroll. 64pp. 0-486-41582-1

SELECTED CANTERBURY TALES, Geoffrey Chaucer. 144pp. 0-486-28241-4

THE RIME OF THE ANCIENT MARINER AND OTHER POEMS, Samuel Taylor Coleridge. 80pp. 0-486-27266-4

THE CAVALIER POETS: An Anthology, Thomas Crofts (ed.). 80pp. 0-486-28766-1

SELECTED POEMS, Emily Dickinson. 64pp. 0-486-26466-1

SELECTED POEMS, John Donne. 96pp. 0-486-27788-7

SELECTED POEMS, Paul Laurence Dunbar. 80pp. 0-486-29980-5

"THE WASTE LAND" AND OTHER POEMS, T. S. Eliot. 64pp. (Available in U.S. only.) 0-486-40061-1

THE RUBÁIYÁT OF OMAR KHAYYÁM: FIRST AND FIFTH EDITIONS, Edward FitzGerald. 64pp. 0-486-26467-X

A BOY'S WILL AND NORTH OF BOSTON, Robert Frost. 112pp. (Available in U.S. only.) 0-486-26866-7

THE ROAD NOT TAKEN AND OTHER POEMS, Robert Frost. 64pp. (Available in U.S. only.) 0-486-27550-7

THE GARDEN OF HEAVEN: POEMS OF HAFIZ, Hafiz. 112pp. 0-486-43161-4

HARDY'S SELECTED POEMS, Thomas Hardy. 80pp. 0-486-28753-X

A SHROPSHIRE LAD, A. E. Housman. 64pp. 0-486-26468-8

LYRIC POEMS, John Keats. 80pp. 0-486-26871-3

GUNGA DIN AND OTHER FAVORITE POEMS, Rudyard Kipling. 80pp. 0-486-26471-8

SNAKE AND OTHER POEMS, D. H. Lawrence. 64pp. 0-486-40647-4

DOVER · THRIFT · EDITIONS

POETRY

THE CONGO AND OTHER POEMS, Vachel Lindsay. 96pp. 0-486-27272-9

EVANGELINE AND OTHER POEMS, Henry Wadsworth Longfellow. 64pp. 0-486-28255-4

FAVORITE POEMS, Henry Wadsworth Longfellow. 96pp. 0-486-27273-7

"TO HIS COY MISTRESS" AND OTHER POEMS, Andrew Marvell. 64pp. 0-486-29544-3

SPOON RIVER ANTHOLOGY, Edgar Lee Masters. 144pp. 0-486-27275-3

SELECTED POEMS, Claude McKay. 80pp. 0-486-40876-0

RENASCENCE AND OTHER POEMS, Edna St. Vincent Millay. 64pp. (Not available in Europe or the United Kingdom) 0-486-26873-X

SELECTED POEMS, John Milton. 128pp. 0-486-27554-X

CIVIL WAR POETRY: An Anthology, Paul Negri (ed.). 128pp. 0-486-29883-3

ENGLISH VICTORIAN POETRY: AN ANTHOLOGY, Paul Negri (ed.). 256pp. 0-486-40425-0

GREAT SONNETS, Paul Negri (ed.). 96pp. 0-486-28052-7

THE RAVEN AND OTHER FAVORITE POEMS, Edgar Allan Poe. 64pp. 0-486-26685-0

ESSAY ON MAN AND OTHER POEMS, Alexander Pope. 128pp. 0-486-28053-5

EARLY POEMS, Ezra Pound. 80pp. (Available in U.S. only.) 0-486-28745-9

GREAT POEMS BY AMERICAN WOMEN: An Anthology, Susan L. Rattiner (ed.). 224pp. (Available in U.S. only.) 0-486-40164-2

GOBLIN MARKET AND OTHER POEMS, Christina Rossetti. 64pp. 0-486-28055-1

CHICAGO POEMS, Carl Sandburg. 80pp. 0-486-28057-8

CORNHUSKERS, Carl Sandburg. 157pp. 0-486-41409-4

COMPLETE SONNETS, William Shakespeare. 80pp. 0-486-26686-9

SELECTED POEMS, Percy Bysshe Shelley. 128pp. 0-486-27558-2

AFRICAN-AMERICAN POETRY: An Anthology, 1773–1930, Joan R. Sherman (ed.). 96pp. 0-486-29604-0

100 BEST-LOVED POEMS, Philip Smith (ed.). 96pp. 0-486-28553-7

NATIVE AMERICAN SONGS AND POEMS: An Anthology, Brian Swann (ed.). 64pp. 0-486-29450-1

SELECTED POEMS, Alfred Lord Tennyson. 112pp. 0-486-27282-6

AENEID, Vergil (Publius Vergilius Maro). 256pp. 0-486-28749-1

CHRISTMAS CAROLS: COMPLETE VERSES, Shane Weller (ed.). 64pp. 0-486-27397-0

GREAT LOVE POEMS, Shane Weller (ed.). 128pp. 0-486-27284-2

CIVIL WAR POETRY AND PROSE, Walt Whitman. 96pp. 0-486-28507-3

SELECTED POEMS, Walt Whitman. 128pp. 0-486-26878-0

THE BALLAD OF READING GAOL AND OTHER POEMS, Oscar Wilde. 64pp. 0-486-27072-6

EARLY POEMS, William Carlos Williams. 64pp. (Available in U.S. only.) 0-486-29294-0

FAVORITE POEMS, William Wordsworth. 80pp. 0-486-27073-4

WORLD WAR ONE BRITISH POETS: Brooke, Owen, Sassoon, Rosenberg, and Others, Candace Ward (ed.). (Available in U.S. only.) 0-486-29568-0

EARLY POEMS, William Butler Yeats. 128pp. 0-486-27808-5

"EASTER, 1916" AND OTHER POEMS, William Butler Yeats. 80pp. (Not available in Europe or United Kingdom.) 0-486-29771-3

DOVER·THRIFT·EDITIONS

PLAYS

LIFE IS A DREAM, Pedro Calderón de la Barca. 96pp. 0-486-42124-4

H. M. S. PINAFORE, William Schwenck Gilbert. 64pp. 0-486-41114-1

THE MIKADO, William Schwenck Gilbert. 64pp. 0-486-27268-0

SHE STOOPS TO CONQUER, Oliver Goldsmith. 80pp. 0-486-26867-5

THE LOWER DEPTHS, Maxim Gorky. 80pp. 0-486-41115-X

A DOLL'S HOUSE, Henrik Ibsen. 80pp. 0-486-27062-9

GHOSTS, Henrik Ibsen. 64pp. 0-486-29852-3

HEDDA GABLER, Henrik Ibsen. 80pp. 0-486-26469-6

PEER GYNT, Henrik Ibsen. 144pp. 0-486-42686-6

THE WILD DUCK, Henrik Ibsen. 96pp. 0-486-41116-8

VOLPONE, Ben Jonson. 112pp. 0-486-28049-7

DR. FAUSTUS, Christopher Marlowe. 64pp. 0-486-28208-2

TAMBURLAINE, Christopher Marlowe. 128pp. 0-486-42125-2

THE IMAGINARY INVALID, Molière. 96pp. 0-486-43789-2

THE MISANTHROPE, Molière. 64pp. 0-486-27065-3

RIGHT YOU ARE, IF YOU THINK YOU ARE, Luigi Pirandello. 64pp. (Not available in Europe or United Kingdom.) 0-486-29576-1

SIX CHARACTERS IN SEARCH OF AN AUTHOR, Luigi Pirandello. 64pp. (Not available in Europe or United Kingdom.) 0-486-29992-9

PHÈDRE, Jean Racine. 64pp. 0-486-41927-4

HANDS AROUND, Arthur Schnitzler. 64pp. 0-486-28724-6

ANTONY AND CLEOPATRA, William Shakespeare. 128pp. 0-486-40062-X

AS YOU LIKE IT, William Shakespeare. 80pp. 0-486-40432-3

HAMLET, William Shakespeare. 128pp. 0-486-27278-8

HENRY IV, William Shakespeare. 96pp. 0-486-29584-2

JULIUS CAESAR, William Shakespeare. 80pp. 0-486-26876-4

KING LEAR, William Shakespeare. 112pp. 0-486-28058-6

LOVE'S LABOUR'S LOST, William Shakespeare. 64pp. 0-486-41929-0

MACBETH, William Shakespeare. 96pp. 0-486-27802-6

MEASURE FOR MEASURE, William Shakespeare. 96pp. 0-486-40889-2

THE MERCHANT OF VENICE, William Shakespeare. 96pp. 0-486-28492-1

A MIDSUMMER NIGHT'S DREAM, William Shakespeare. 80pp. 0-486-27067-X

MUCH ADO ABOUT NOTHING, William Shakespeare. 80pp. 0-486-28272-4

OTHELLO, William Shakespeare. 112pp. 0-486-29097-2

RICHARD III, William Shakespeare. 112pp. 0-486-28747-5

ROMEO AND JULIET, William Shakespeare. 96pp. 0-486-27557-4

THE TAMING OF THE SHREW, William Shakespeare. 96pp. 0-486-29765-9

THE TEMPEST, William Shakespeare. 96pp. 0-486-40658-X

TWELFTH NIGHT; OR, WHAT YOU WILL, William Shakespeare. 80pp. 0-486-29290-8

ARMS AND THE MAN, George Bernard Shaw. 80pp. (Not available in Europe or United Kingdom.) 0-486-26476-9

HEARTBREAK HOUSE, George Bernard Shaw. 128pp. (Not available in Europe or United Kingdom.) 0-486-29291-6

PYGMALION, George Bernard Shaw. 96pp. (Available in U.S. only.) 0-486-28222-8

THE RIVALS, Richard Brinsley Sheridan. 96pp. 0-486-40433-1

THE SCHOOL FOR SCANDAL, Richard Brinsley Sheridan. 96pp. 0-486-26687-7

ANTIGONE, Sophocles. 64pp. 0-486-27804-2

OEDIPUS AT COLONUS, Sophocles. 64pp. 0-486-40659-8

OEDIPUS REX, Sophocles. 64pp. 0-486-26877-2

DOVER·THRIFT·EDITIONS

PLAYS

ELECTRA, Sophocles. 64pp. 0-486-28482-4

MISS JULIE, August Strindberg. 64pp. 0-486-27281-8

THE PLAYBOY OF THE WESTERN WORLD AND RIDERS TO THE SEA, J. M. Synge. 80pp. 0-486-27562-0

THE DUCHESS OF MALFI, John Webster. 96pp. 0-486-40660-1

THE IMPORTANCE OF BEING EARNEST, Oscar Wilde. 64pp. 0-486-26478-5

LADY WINDERMERE'S FAN, Oscar Wilde. 64pp. 0-486-40078-6

BOXED SETS

FAVORITE JANE AUSTEN NOVELS: *Pride and Prejudice, Sense and Sensibility* and *Persuasion* (Complete and Unabridged), Jane Austen. 800pp. 0-486-29748-9

BEST WORKS OF MARK TWAIN: Four Books, Dover. 624pp. 0-486-40226-6

EIGHT GREAT GREEK TRAGEDIES: Six Books, Dover. 480pp. 0-486-40203-7

FIVE GREAT ENGLISH ROMANTIC POETS, Dover. 496pp. 0-486-27893-X

GREAT AFRICAN-AMERICAN WRITERS: Seven Books, Dover. 704pp. 0-486-29995-3

GREAT WOMEN POETS: 4 Complete Books, Dover. 256pp. (Available in U.S. only.) 0-486-28388-7

MASTERPIECES OF RUSSIAN LITERATURE: Seven Books, Dover. 880pp. 0-486-40665-2

SIX GREAT AMERICAN POETS: Poems by Poe, Dickinson, Whitman, Longfellow, Frost, and Millay, Dover. 512pp. (Available in U.S. only.) 0-486-27425-X

FAVORITE NOVELS AND STORIES: Four Complete Books, Jack London. 568pp. 0-486-42216-X

FIVE GREAT SCIENCE FICTION NOVELS, H. G. Wells. 640pp. 0-486-43978-X

FIVE GREAT PLAYS OF SHAKESPEARE, Dover. 496pp. 0-486-27892-1

TWELVE PLAYS BY SHAKESPEARE, William Shakespeare. 1,173pp. 0-486-44336-1